100 years of Mancheste Primary School 1907-2007

Sketch by Grady Kempson Year 6

Compiled by Glenn Piper 2007

Contents	Page
Introduction	4
Miscellaneous photographs	5
Chapter 1 The Early Years 1907-1918	8
Chapter 2 The Inter War Years 1919-1938	20
Chapter 3 The War Years 1939-1945	37
Chapter 4 The Post War Years 1946-1960	43
Chapter 5 The Sixties and Beyond 1961-1981	57
Chapter 6 The Last Decades of the Century 1981-1999	76
Chapter 7 The New Millennium 2000-2007	84
Appendix Alphabetical list of pupils at Manchester Road School in 1907	86
Thanks	94
Appendix 1-copies of letters received from ex-pupils and teachers.	**Phylis Walstow** **Miss Lawrence** **Sheilagh Schofield** **May Trill** **Alison Cooke** **Ray Charter** **Trevor Bevan** **Sharman Birtles** **Sara Mannion**
Appendix 2-	**Prize lists for 1966,1969 and 1970** **Concert programme 1969**

Introduction.

2007 is our Centenary year when we celebrate 100 years of life in Manchester Road Primary School. It is an ideal time to look back and read about the experience of pupils and teachers in the past. I hope this will be of interest not just to ex-pupils but also to anyone with an interest in local history and genealogy. A lot of the log book entries are very mundane and a lot relate to attendance and staff absences. I have tried to pick out entries that will be of interest to readers. As family history is an increasingly popular hobby I am also including a full list of the pupils at the school when it opened in 1907. This gives their full name, year of birth and name of parent/guardian.

Droylsden has had a long history of providing education for its citizens. In fact, many of the staff and pupils of Manchester Road in 1907 came from the old British National School on Queen Street. The Headmaster of the new Junior School, Mr George Dawson was the head of the Queen Street School. This would explain the remarkable discovery made at the back of the store cupboard by Mr Piper in 2001. Underneath a pile of old boxes and stock paper were some old log books. This included the log book of the Queen Street School, Droylsden 1864-1907. This exciting discovery gives us a glimpse back into Victorian education in Droylsden. Extracts from this have been typed and there is a surname index available. The original log book has been deposited at Tameside Archives for preservation and for future generations to study.

You have the opportunity to read parts of these archives in the comfort of your own home.

We have scanned the original Queen Street log book 1864-1907, the Manchester Road Admission Registers for 1907 and the Infant and Junior School log book for Manchester Road School 1907-1918. These are available to purchase on one CD. Full details on our website www.manchesterroad.org.uk

1904 Queen Street National School

Manchester Road School. Date unknown.

Timetable. Date unknown

Senior Boys timetable. Date unknown

Chapter 1 The Early Years 1907-1918

INFANTS
1907
Headteacher   Miss Smith
November 22nd. A party of Negroes from Africa gave an entertainment this afternoon, consisting of songs etc.
November 25th. A dense fog prevails this morning, causing the attendance to be poor.
December 19th. School visited by a deputation from Preston. Close this afternoon for a fortnight. The children took home with them, Christmas cards which had been coloured.
1908
January 17th. Miss Hudson is still absent. I have kept Eva Proctor, a pupil teacher from her class, to help today... Stanley Beard, a child of four years, fell in the playground yesterday morning and cut his face.
January 21st. Eva Proctor gave a lesson in stick laying this afternoon, which I criticised.
May 22nd. The children sang the national anthem and waved the Union Jack. Many of the children bought flags with them. They gave three cheers for the King and were dismissed. As they went out a thunderstorm came on, and they had to shelter in the cloakroom.
June 16th. Mrs Wigley bought Margaret this morning. I took her under protest, as she has a copious discharge from her ears. However, I told her mother that if the smell became a nuisance I should send her home.
October 1st. Jesse Rathbone starts today. Born 12th of December 1889.

1909.
April 6th. The attendance is very bad indeed, as so many children have bad colds. In class three, only 29 children are present this morning.
May 18th. Have lighted the fire in the babies room, as I think it is too cold for them without.
October 13th. A very stormy morning and a very poor attendance.
November 23rd. Some of the children look so starved that I sent for some milk and heated it for the ones who I thought had insufficient food.
November 24th. A great amount of sickness among the children. I gave out clothes sent by Mrs Beard and Mrs Hoyland. They are a great boon to some ill clad children.
1910.
January 24th. A very stormy morning. It's snowing and a very difficult to walk. We were all pleased to see a fire in the teacher's room as well as bright fires in the babies room.
March 1st. Alec Robertson has had a leave of absence from school until after the Easter holidays and Gladys Green until after the summer holiday. Mrs Harper gave the leave. She also said that the children with ringworm might be in school if they wore a cap or a bonnet.
July 14th. One of the children bought us a tortoise which her father had given her to bring. The children are pleased to have it. They were quite distressed

by the death of one that we had last year. It died about Easter. We had it but 4 years.

July 22nd. I caned a boy rather severely today. He took a book out of the cupboard and carried it home under his jersey. As it is not the first time he has taken what did not belong to him, I gave him two strokes on each hand.

One of the earliest pictures of Manchester Road children c1910

1911.

January 23rd. Attendance still poor. Many children have had colds. The babies are having a doll's house made of the orange box that had the Christmas oranges in. They are much pleased with it.

May 1st. Sent Eveline Cropps home, having heard that there is a case of scarlet fever in her home. I thought it wise to do so. She came back this afternoon with a note from her mother to the effect that the doctor said is quite safe for her to come to school.

December 19th. We had no usual party. The teachers have decorated the hall and the baby's room very beautifully. The children came at six o'clock and used a class of room for coats. For an hour we had an entertainment provided by the different classes. The mince pies were taken round and the lights lowered so that the children could see the lights from a snow scene.... after this Santa Claus came in, carrying a sack full of toys on his back and every child had a toy. They then said goodnight and went home. An orange was given to every child as he or she passed out.

1912.

May 7th. A child in class two is leaving today -- going to Canada.

1913.

February 20th. The weather is very severe and many children are ill. Called to see Herbert Chipchase. He is getting on well, has had the stitches taken out and is making great progress.

May 9th. Sent a boy home this morning, who has a very bad eye. The child was in great pain, but did not want to stay at home.

June 27th. Copy of Her Majesty Inspector's report. There is much to praise in the work done in the school. The physical side of the instruction is carefully considered and much brightness is to be found in the games, and in some of the dances. The speech training is still rather too formal, though many children are ready to tell stories and to respond to questions.... the children know the sounds of the letters and the old build up words readily... in number it is felt that the scheme in the past has been too advanced... the teachers are working very well indeed. The children are also working well, and all fairly responsive. It is suggested that a rather lighter hand on the reins in every class would be beneficial to the children.

July 21st. There is much sickness -- several children have whooping cough, and there are cases of chickenpox and measles.

1914.

January 19th. I had notice this morning of a case of scarlet fever. I found a child from the house in school, so sent her home.

February 20th. Several children have sore eyes, and therefore cannot attend.

May 4th. Many fresh cases of measles have developed during the weekend. Willie Fish has come this afternoon, and as they have measles still in the house I have sent him home.

August 3rd. I, **Annie Buckley Wood**, commenced duties as head mistress of this school.

1915

Miss Ethel Clough commenced duties this morning. She has been transferred from Failsworth. Date of birth, 1892.

1916

May 24th. This afternoon, we celebrated Empire Day. The last two lessons of the afternoon session were devoted to the celebration. The children brought flags and we went out into the playground, where each class sang an Empire song. Then we saluted the flag and the children marched around the playground. After cheering for the King and gallant defenders, the National Anthem was sung. The children went home at 3:45 p.m.

1917

May 24th. This afternoon, we celebrated Empire Day in a small way. Almost every child bought a flag and we went out into the playground and sang the Empire song.

1918.

March 6th. The school was to be closed for the next two days. The teachers are attending at the council offices to help with the issue of the meat rationing cards. The average attendances 209.

March 13th. Today we had an air raid alarm practice. The gong sounded the alarm at 11:45 a.m., and immediately all work stopped and the children went home as quickly as possible, not stopping to put on hats or coats. The children were very orderly, and the streets were quickly cleared.

Alex Ellison

JUNIORS
1907
December 2. Mr J. Thomason will be absent all this week, by permission attending the certificate examination.

December 19. Have given the last three weeks to examinations of the classes as far as the absence of teachers are allowed time for the work. The results show that all the teachers have conscientiously gone through all the world appointed -- there are of course some weaknesses, especially in the lower standards, but there is one consolation even in this -- the failures are chiefly among the children who have been admitted from neighbouring schools, (Manchester schools), and not from the old British schools.

In measuring the results, the fact needs to be kept in mind; each week of the past three months has witnessed the advent of new children.

1908
January 7th. Mrs Caldwell came this morning to make a complaint about Mr Brierley, punishing her boy for dullness during an arithmetic lesson.

January 16th. Received a note from Mr Entwistle 100, Kershaw Street, complaining about Mr Brierley's treatment of his daughter Lizzie.

February 21st. Mr Morris gave a science object lesson on alcohol, from 10 to 10:45 a.m.

April 28. Mr Hilton, class four, was accidentally knocked down while at play in the schoolyard, and had his left arm broken.

May 21. An unfortunate mishap came to a girl in class 38 -- Emily White. Mrs Wormald gave a push to call her from inattention, and the girl knocked on her forehead against the edge of the next desk, making a cut three quarters of an inch long. Every attention was given to the girl.

May 22. Special history lesson on the empire given by each teacher, and half holiday in afternoon in celebration of Empire Day.

July the sixth. Mrs Rose made complaints about punishment of her boy -- Edward -- by Miss Barlow.

July 29. Albert Taylor. P.T has passed the matriculation exam. Second division.

August the fifth. Percy Newton and old scholar began service as pupil teacher.

October 1. Mrs Rush and myself absent in the afternoon. Attended the wedding of Miss Effie M Brown, who, until this date, was on the staff of the infant department.

October 20. Mr Bailey called in the afternoon to complain about Mr Brierley's punishment of his daughter, Agnes.

November the 17th Mrs Warburton, again complained about her daughter being struck on the hand by Mr Brierley. Spoke to Mr Brierley.

December the second received a letter of complaint from Mr Hargreaves concerning Mr Brierley's treatment of Harry Hargreaves.

1909

January 15. Children photographed on this date. Social for the first two classes in the evening.

January 22. Average attendance fallen 13 below last week. Five away because of scarlet fever in the families.

February 18. One of the boys in class five earlier (J..Docker) got a nasty fall in attempting to get on a tram after it had started.

March 12. Saw Mr Knott by appointment concerning the dissatisfaction I have with Mr Brierley.

May 3. The attendance is breaking down a little through the advent of mumps in certain families.

June. Copy of the reports made by her Majesty's Inspector. The school has been at work in new commodious premises for about 18 months. Satisfactory teaching is given by an adequate staff, whose aim is not only to give solid instruction, but to cultivate ready mindedness in their scholars.

July 1. Commencement of the New Year. Staff.
Mr George Dawson.
Mr Brierley.
John Thomason.
Agnes Stead.
Annie White
Gamal Etchells.
Walter Rushworth.
Annie Wormald
Ada rush.
Mabel Barlow.
Zoe white.
Marian Lea.
Percy Newton.

September 9th. Sergeant Major Wright, inspected the drill in the afternoon.
October 1st. The following passed merit examination.
John Barrow.
Joshua Smith.
John Day.

George Birch.
Annie Holland
Agnes Hartley.
October 21st. Mr W. Rushworth absent in the afternoon. Visiting a friend in the infirmary.
December 24th. Closed the school at noon for Christmas holidays. Mrs A Stead left on this date, she has been a good and faithful teacher.

1910
January 10th. Reopened the school. Miss Marian Walker commenced duties as assistant in place of Mrs Stead. Number present 420. Absent 47.
January 19th. Mrs Wormald absent by permission. Taking her boy John to a Halifax orphanage.
February 1st. Mr Brierley returned. Spoke to Miss Barlow about, not keeping the timetable quite strictly enough, and her inclination to teach too much from the desk.
February 8th. Mr Barlow came to lay serious complaints against the treatment of his son John by Mr Brierley.
February 22. Spoke to Mr Brierley concerning the punishment of Ethel Oldham, and called attention to the fact that I'd put my instructions before him in writing, as regards manner of punishments. In the afternoon, Mrs Allen came to complain about May being hit.
April 6. Mrs White came to complain about her boy Harry having been struck on the hand by his teacher. Mr W. Rushworth.
April 8th. Had to interfere with Mr Brierley for mercilessly hitting a boy. John Evans. Boy says this was simply for not been able to answer something. Mrs Evans called in the afternoon to make complaint about this.
June 14 Mr G. Etchells gave permission to be absent in order to attend the funeral of a niece.
June 22 notified that Harry Hibbert has gained a junior scholarship. Percy Newton, pupil teacher, has passed the examination with distinction in English.
September 6. Reopen the school. All teachers present. Attendance 444.
Miss Howarth, and Edward Joyce entered upon their work is pupil teachers.
September 22 received results of merit examination. Passed, Edward Ridgeway, Harry Sumner, Harry Hibbert, Ethel Moores.
October 26, punished four boys -- Richmond, Binns, Taylor and Shirley for playing truant previous afternoon. Appear to have been led away by a bigger boy not attending school.

1911
February 17th. There is much sickness -- many cases of eczema and several cases of scarlet fever have been notified.
April 3rd. Gave permission to Mr Thomas to be absent for purpose of the census taking.
September 5. Staff at reopening. Mr Dawson. Mr Brierley. Mrs Wormald. Mrs A Smith. Mrs A Stead. Miss Walker. Mr Etchells. Mr W. Rushworth. Mrs A Rush. Miss M Lea.
Pupil teachers, Edward Joyce, Hilda Hayworth, Norman Tonge.
September 12 this afternoon over 60 boys absented themselves. On strike, they said. Wrote a postcard to father of each striker
September 21 received results of merit certificate exam. 15 passed. Hubert Dickens. Ernest Sheaton. Fred Tomlinson. Gladys Docker. Lolita Townall.

Alf Collins. James Newton. Herb Allman. Beatrice Hulley. Gladys Day. David Hopkin's. Wilfred Cooke. Kathleen Buckley. Mary Watson. Louie Crossley.

A pre war photograph

1912
March 6, Miss Lea went home at 11 suffering from sore throat. Gave permission from Mrs Stead, to be absent in afternoon to attend the bazaar.
March 12 spoke to Mr Rushworth and Mrs Rush about talking to each other during marching of classes to rooms.
March 29. Attendance has been falling all week, in consequence of the shortage of fuel in many houses, through colliers strike.
July 18, one of the boys in class 4B was interred today. Accidentally drowned in canal last Thursday evening. Name Thomas Newby.
September 9, present 459. Miss B. Snowden commenced duties as assistant in place of Mrs Wormald, whose engagement ended August 31.
September 24 attendance 488. Results of the merit certificate examination held in May. Kelly Hargreaves. Lucy Matthews. Ada Leah. W. Wood. Jason Marshall. Eva Pearson. Charles Mellor. Harold Burns. John Maddison. All passed.

1913
April 1, Miss Hilda Hayworth commenced her engagement as uncertified teacher. Since July last she has been an assistant in the Audenshaw School.
September 8. Mr W. Rushworth not present, on account of having accepted, a place in Manchester training college as a student for two years.
November 10, Miss Nora Park came as a supply teacher.
November 14 Attendance dropped much during week through increase of sickness. Several fresh cases of scarlet fever.
November 17, Mr A. Morris, of the band of Hope union gave two lessons on

alcohol to upper standards.
November 26 copy of inspection report.
The instruction is systematic and conscientiously given. The headmaster is free to give careful supervision, and the staff are working well. The result of the teaching are, on the whole, creditable and in some respects praiseworthy. While there is a liberal supply of good literature, and the older children would appear interested in it, it is advisable that more silent reading be taken by them. The composition in the upper classes might be a more varied and interesting character. In the lower section, the development of speech and storytelling calls for very much more consideration than is at present given to it. Oral lessons in geography, history, and elementary science have been very successful. The children's sympathies have been fully engaged and their individual interests secured. The dramatised reproductions of history had been interesting, and instructive to the younger children. Needlework is practical and of a satisfactory character, special care being devoted to mending and making garments. Handwriting is very good and much of the drawing, though it will be advisable to take more crayon work in the lower section, deserves special mention.

1914.
January 8, Mr.Perfect returned in afternoon, after three half days absence through insomnia.
April 20 received notice that Mr Brierley wants to be absent all week through the advent of scarlet fever in the family.
May 19, scholarship result. Christopher Witham. Mr S. Perfect absent -- nervous dyspepsia.
June 30, average attendance for year 425.
Copy of inspection report. The playground surface has been repaired and could use is now made of the borders around it. These are planted with seeds and plants brought by the children and tended by the older boys. They are interested in taking care of the plants, which should provide material for observation lessons and for drawing. It is a pleasure to note the great improvement made in drawing during the past year. In composition, both oral and written there is still room for much improvement. Teachers and children are working very well, and the staff of the school is very satisfactory.
July 24 received merit examination results. Nine passed. Florence Silson. Doris Ogden. James Docker. Norman Hutchinson. Stanley Armstrong. Mark Kendrick. Albert Gee? Harry Leah. Christopher Witham.
October 15, Mrs A J Smith absent. Reported later that she had contracted scarlet fever.
December 14, absent in morning with indisposition (neurological sleeplessness?)

1915.
February 16, Mr Perfect returned. Says he had an attack of nervous dyspepsia.
June 24. Mr Seddon came to complain about the punishment given to his daughter Emily by Mr Brierley. He has removed both girls (Emily and Louie) from the school.
July 8. Two former pupils and one present pupil appear in the Manchester scholarship list. Kathleen Copestake. Ruth Blackley. Arthur Watson.
July 22, Sam Lloyd has been granted a free admission scholarship to Burley

St. Nora Copestake, has won a £10 scholarship and Jessie Copestake, a bursary.

September 28 results of merit certificate exam. William Fishwick. Eve Hutchinson. Shirley Stanley. Emily Seddon. Conny Hayes. Mary White.

October 29. Mrs A Smith leaves on this date, in consequence of removal to Leeds. She has had a long connection with the school as a scholar, pupil teacher and assistant teacher, and has been a most faithful servant, and leaves with the good wishes of the children and her fellow teachers.

November 9. Wet morning -- many children absent. Mr Perfect, absent in morning. Says important business.

November 12, Mr Perfect finishes today on account of enlistment.

November 22, Mr Perfect returned -- sent away from army as unequal to the strain of training. Miss Lea absent -- bruised hand through fall.

December 6, Mr R Barlow and old scholar and pupil teacher of the school has just completed his BA degree.

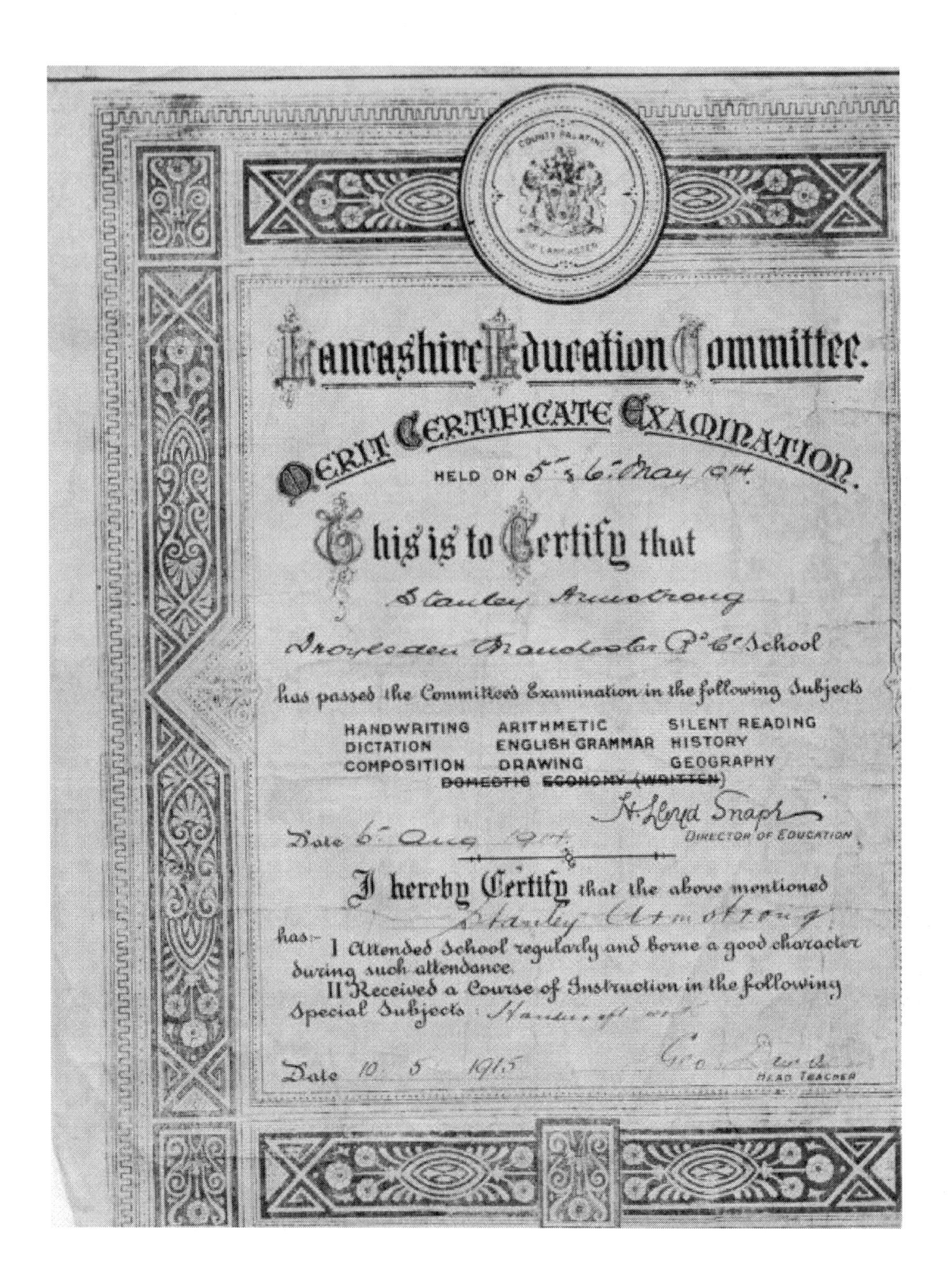

1916.
February 2. Mr Perfect at 12 o'clock said he should be a little late in the afternoon -- he had some business in town.
February 11th Completed today, 50 years service as a teacher In Droylsden schools having commenced as a monitor in the Droylsden British school on February the 12th 1866. Signed.**George Dawson.**
May 30 Mrs Rush absent during morning session. Says seeing her soldier son off.
June 20 Miss H Haworth absent -- enlarged tonsils.
July 1. Present staff.

George Dawson.
John Thomasson.
John Perfect.
G Etchells
Marian Lea.
Marian Walker.
Edith Park.
Mrs Delia Curran.
Mrs Ada Rush.
Miss H Haworth

September 5, children photographed in the afternoon.

October 6 Been endeavouring to secure an improvement in the collar wearing in lower classes.

December 1st. Absent in afternoon attending the funeral of a soldier -- son of an old friend.

1917.

February 12th. Commenced a War savings club for the children and friends. Weeks deposits were £102.

March 9th. The severe weather has reduced the attendance this week. Parents have of late shown a keen desire to get their children to work half-time or full-time at the very earliest opportunity (legal). This arises from two causes -- the demand for labour and the newspaper rumours of the likely raising of age from leaving school.

April 2, as a blizzard was raging this morning during the time children were coming to school, the attendance was thereby very much affected. 205 present out of 409. Miss Park, bravely walked all the way from Dukinfield.

May the 11th during the next two weeks, the main lessons will be made to bear on the food questions -- and the view of creating the right atmosphere for the economy campaign -- in accordance with instructions from the county council.

June 25, the subscriptions to the war savings bank now amount to £254.

June 27. Mr Morris of the Band of Hope Union gave lectures on alcohol.

October 31, Miss Hilda Haworth, left on this date to take up duties in a school nearer her home (Hurst). She has been a good and faithful assistance.

November 14. Mrs Halliwell (nee Barlow), commenced duties as a supply assistant in place of Miss Haworth. Mrs Jones came to complain of Mr Perfect, striking her boy in the face during the dinner hour yesterday. As I have done on several former occasions, I told Mr Perfect, that such cases should be reported to me.

November 20, called Mr Perfect to complain about the punishment of the smallest boy in its class, Whittaker. He said it was for inattention. I then pointed out that he talked at the desk too much. As he became insulting I told him to go to his place and leave the school. This he said he should not do.

1918.

March 1. Mrs Halliwell completed her services as temporary assistant today. Her place is taken by Miss Nora Farran(?)

April 23 St. George's Day. Appropriate lessons given. Sale of flags for wounded horses funds (£1.0.8).

April 30, War savings fund has this week reached £1000.

May 10 sale of flowers for national home for children, £1.0.8.

May 17, completed the planting of potatoes at the school garden. Some 200 brought by the children themselves.

May 27, Miss M. Walker, absent in afternoon asked permission to do some shopping, on account the death of her brother-in-law in France.

June 5. Twice this afternoon, Mr Perfect has defied my instructions.

July 2. This morning, 138 children absent. Some through the epidemic of influenza, which is afflicting surrounding districts.

July 3, receive notice from medical officers of health to close the school because of the spreading of influenza. This is the first reason in my experience that the school has been closed for an epidemic attack.

September 2, Mr Perfect concluded his engagement on August 31.

September 10th, Mrs Rose Leigh (Rushworth) commenced duty as temporary assistant in place of Mr Perfect who resigned.

November 7th, received notice from the medical officer of health that all Droylsden schools were to close at once on account of the influenza epidemic. This notice was repeated week by week until the advent of the Christmas holidays.

Asher Ahmed. Year 6

Chapter 2 The inter war years 1919-1938

INFANTS
1919.
September 1st. The school reopened this morning with a very fair attendance. All the teachers have returned to duties and several new children have been admitted during the summer holidays I have been married and my name is now **Annie Buckley Warburton.**
1920
July 15th. The staff of the school. Miss M Carter, Miss M Hudson, Miss H Casey, Miss F Vernon, Mrs E Wainwright.
1921
Staff of the Infant School

November 11th. The children assembled in the hall the morning just before 11 o'clock and stood silently for two minutes. Then they sang one verse of Rudyard Kipling's "God of our Father."

1923.
January 31st. Nurse Hutchinson visited the school this morning and examined the children. While going home this afternoon, Elsie Collier, a child in second class was knocked down by a motor car, but not seriously hurt.
April 9th. School reopened this morning, when all of the staff and 152 children were present out of 187 on our books.
April 26th. The school will be closed on this date, to celebrate the wedding of her Royal Highness the Duke of York.

August 1st. The staff for the coming year is as follows;.Miss Schofield, Miss Vernon, Mrs Casey, Miss Carter, Mrs Wainwright.
November 1st. Miss Carter is absent from school this morning, owing to the presence of a fish bone in her throat.
1924.
April 11th. The Headteacher will be absent from school on this date and will not be present again until school reopens after Easter, having been summoned to Whitehall to be interviewed by the Board of Education in connection with the position on the Inspectorate of Elementary schools, and afterwards join in an educational expedition to Pisa, Florence and Rome.
1925.
April 9th. The Headteacher is absent from school this morning having received official permission to join an educational tour to Milan, Venice, Como and Lucerne.
April 20th. Cases of scarlet fever, whooping cough and chickenpox are reported in nearly every class.

Pauline Morgan c1925 by the sand box in Mr Morley's class. Pauline remembers the following children in the class;Kenneth Townsend,Lillian Hamlet,Harry Camel,Keith Buckley,Ronnie Priestnall, Edwin Dewsnap,Eric Evans,Charlie Schofield,Alan Horsfield,Kenneth White, Joe Taylor,Hilda Whittaker,Alan Readet,Margaret Hatton,Thomas Lothian,Sylvia Hetherington,Edna Carter,Joan Swindells,Lucy Anderson,Lily Schofield.
1926.
April 1st. The Headteacher will be absent this morning having received official permission to join an educational tour to Avignon.
July 12th. On this date my service as Headteacher of Manchester Rd Council School is completed, signed **Jessie Rathbone**. **Annie Heys** took charge of this department at Manchester Road School this morning.

1927.

November 30th. Their attendance this month has been very poor owing to measles, fever and diphtheria. Dr Conk, the school medical officer has visited the school this week, investigating the cases of diphtheria.

1928.
March 14th. During the past year, the staff have organised two whist drives. The proceeds have been devoted to a Christmas treat for the children, the purchasing of a rocking horse for the babies, and for schoolbooks for the children's library etc.
July 18th. There will be a slight change in the timetable this morning so that the children may listen to Mr Ward on Canada. Yesterday, many of the children with the staff visited the pictures at 4:15 p.m. to see a film on Canada.
1929.
June 6th. Two new pictures -- the "Blue Boy" and a "Boy and the Rabbits" have been hung in the hall in place of others not suitable. These pictures have been purchased by funds raised from teachers efforts.
August 2nd. School closed at noon today to commemorate the winning of 2 cups by the senior girls. Yesterday an accident occurred in the cloakroom, and this morning, we found out that the child, Joan Swindells has broken her leg. She was wearing clogs and slipped on the concrete floor.
September 18th. This morning, the electric light was used for the first time.
October 1st. This afternoon, William Bolton, slipped in the yard on his way to the lavatories and splintered his elbow bone.

1930
October 10th copy of Her Majesty Inspectors report. The spirit of the department is good. The headmistress and her staff showed commendable earnestness and industry. The children are much interested in their school activities and show a pleasing confidence in conversation, and in movement within the classrooms....... on the whole, the work in the primary subjects makes creditable progress. The teaching of the top class is stimulating and resourceful.
October 23rd. As the staff were on the point of leaving the building, Ronald Butler returned to school with a trapped finger, which had been damaged by the outer gates of the Boy's Department.
November 10th. During recreation, Leslie Wood fell in the yard and broke his arm.
1931.
January 7th. The attendance is very poor owing to dense fog. This afternoon there were only 99 children present, out of 198.
April 13th. School reopened this morning. 182 children were present. A Decca gramophone has been purchased with the proceeds of a whist drive and dance organised by the staff in March.
1933.
July 14th. Ernest Roscoe, aged seven, fell on the yard during recreation and dislocated his hip. He had previously been warned about rough play, but openly defied his teacher.
1934
November 29th. Royal Wedding. School closed for the day.

Infant photo. Keith Ellerton front row, sitting
1936.
January 21st. His Majesty the King died during the previous night. On arrival at school this morning, the children watched Mr Woodhall hoist the school flag half-mast.
January 28th. School closed for the funeral of his Majesty King George.

July 16th. Olive Salisbury fractured her elbow during playtime.

October 8th. One of the children, Marion Griffin, was knocked down by a corporation bus this morning on the way to school at 9 a.m.. I accompanied her in the ambulance to Ashton district infirmary where she was left for observation.

November 26th. Dorothy Hull broke her arm in the schoolyard before school opened in the afternoon.

1937.

April 8th. Copy of her Majesty Inspector's report. There are 303 children on the roll of this department. It is organised into six classes. Four of the classes have more than 50 children on the roll, the largest number 56 being in the lowest class. Despite these large classes, however, the school was providing a sound training for the children. There is an atmosphere of good order, joy and happiness throughout the school and the headmistress and her staff are to be commended for their industry and interest. The children are receiving a sound preparation for the later school life, and at the same time they were given every opportunity for expressing themselves through creative activities..... one of the outstanding features of the school is the musical training that is being given and the sound introduction to rhythmic work through a percussion band, recently introduced.

December 17th. On entering school this morning we found that thieves had been during the night. All the desks had been forced open and about 10 shillings in money taken. The police had been notified.

1938.

March 8th. This morning during playtime, Donald Tapper, in his temper, bit a boy's hand, bringing blood. He was punished by being strapped.

May 25th. Parents attended this afternoon to see the Empire Pageant.

JUNIORS
1919.

May 30. Today, I conclude my career as a teacher. Have been master of this school since its opening in 1907 and was previously head of the old British school from first of April 1878 to its closing in October 1907. **George Dawson.**

June 2. Today, I commenced duties as temporary headmaster of the school. **John Thomasson.**

July 14 Charles Goodwin, a boy was sent from his class for stubbornness this afternoon after being warned in the morning. I sent him to ask his father or mother to come to the school to see me, but as he had not returned at 4 p.m. I struck off his attendance mark.

July 17th. Today, the school was closed for peace celebration -- 3 days.

September 17th This morning the woodwork teacher did not arrive so the boys were obliged to return to school. Five boys did not arrive at school until 14 minutes past 10 -- nearly half an hour after the first arrived. As they were marked absent a letter was sent to each boy's father, explaining that the absence was due to "lagging"

September 23 three teachers, Miss Park, Miss Lea and Mrs Curran were late this morning (9:10 a.m.). No cars.

September 29, several teachers late this morning owing to the railway strike causing crowded cars. Receive news that two girls (Annie Hodkin and Kelly Strafford) had won scholarships at Fairfield high school for girls.

October 16 Having addressed the teachers on the habit of coming late and its

influence on the scholars, Mrs Rush took exception and spoke unpleasingly.
November 11th, Miss Farran late (9:20 a.m.). Cars delayed. Armistice Day. All children assembled at 11 a.m. for service of silence and remembrance.
December 3, Mrs Rush late this morning (9:10 a.m.) -- said being delayed shopping. I spoke to her and told her that she was not playing a straight game.

1920

January 29th. Very bad wintry morning. Wet snow was falling heavily, and the roads were covered. Consequently, travelling was very bad. 67 children absent. Teachers got to school very well indeed -- only one (Miss Lea) arriving after nine o'clock. She arrived at 9:10 a.m. -- wet through -- having had to walk much of the way.

February 11th. Receive a letter from Miss Park, saying that she was suffering from an internal strain and was ordered to be quite still for a time.

February 26 punished 12 boys (1 stroke each) for playing football in the yard after being warned twice not to do so owing to the damage done to windows and injury to smaller boys.

March 19. Today, the school War Savings Association closes. It opened in 1917, and has raised the sum of £2189.

March 29 a fairly large portion of the boys yard has been underwater since Thursday. The drain seems to be defective. I've sent for the caretaker on two occasions, but on each occasion the caretaker's wife has reported that he was in bed resting.

April 1 present staff.
John Thomasson
A Wignall
M Walker
M Lea
D Curran
E Park
A Murray
G Etchells
A Rush
N Barley

May 12 Mrs Barley again late this morning, 9:40 a.m. -- said current was off.
June 14, Mrs Rush sent home today at 3:15 p.m., suffering from a bad leg. Five boys (A Stores, A Wilkinson, L Naylor, Jas Boyd, Alf Davenport) have accidentally broken a window today through playing with a golf ball. I have asked them to pay 4 pence, to defray the cost. All have now paid.

July 16. Mrs Barley late this morning -- 9:40 a.m. She said the car was delayed, but I pointed out her irregularity during the past few months, and said that I should take more drastic action if such irregularity continued.

September 2nd, Mrs Curran absence today owing to the visit of an uncle from America. Today, Harold Sheard, age 8, was suddenly taken ill and owing to violent convulsions remained unconscious for almost 2 hours before he was taken home by the doctor to his parents. Mrs Rush and Miss Park, deserve great praise for the kind and able assistance so willingly given.

September 21 received letter from Mr Knott saying managers had resolved to transfer Mr A Wignall to Fairfield Road Council School.

November 23. Mrs Hickman and Mrs Barley. Late this morning. Cars

delayed. Addressed teachers on the too frequent habit of being late.
November 25. Mrs Barley, absent this morning. Returned in afternoon. The injury to foot in alighting from tramcar.

1921.

January 26 school closed this afternoon in order that the teachers might attend a Cinematograph demonstration in Denton.

January 31 13 boys playing with a large marble cracked a window today. I have asked them to play 1 and half pence each to defray the cost. All have now paid.

February 14, Mrs E Schofield commenced duty, a supply teacher. William Buckley, has gained admission to the Manchester Grammar School.

March 1st. Mrs Rylance commenced her duty as a temporary teacher in place of Mrs Hickman.

March 10, allowed Mr Etchells to leave school at 2:30 p.m. to attend a bazaar.

March 22, Mrs Rush, absent this afternoon -- left word that she had a bad head.

April 13th, this afternoon, a girl, Hilda Lane, aged 10, was playing in the yard before the afternoon session began. She slipped and fell and owing to the fall damaged her wrist.

April 25. Today Mrs Rylance fainted in her classroom, and had to be sent home at noon for the day.

May 24, many children absent. This is probably in large measure due to the fact today, a free motor trip is being given to the poor children of the district.

May 30, A t the County Police Athletics Sports the school was successful in winning the first prize and Victory Cup in the half mile team race for schoolboys.

June 13, Miss Walker absent today -- severe cold. Mrs Rush did not arrive until 10:25 a.m. Said there was no train service from Liverpool.

July 4th. Mr P Newton, a former scholar and pupil teacher has been successful in gaining a BSC at Manchester University.

July 12th. Three boys (G Stead,Geo Spencer,Jas Whitham) accidentally broke a window today. I have asked them to pay sixpence each to defray the cost. All have now paid.

August 1 staff.
John Thomasson
G Etchells
Marian Walker
Delia Curran
Marian Lea
Edith Park
Delia Rylance
Amy Murray
Ada Rush
Ethel Gee

August 5 school closed for Midsummer holiday -- 4 weeks. During the holiday, the interior of the school is being beautified.

September 30, Mrs Curran completed her engagement as assistant teacher. She has been a good and faithful teacher.

October 10, Miss F. Charnock commenced temporary duty today.

December 12, attendance still very poor, 57 absent. Mr A Hudson, a student in training at the Training College, Erith, Kent, commenced school practice this morning.

December 22, Mr Etchells absent this afternoon, by permission to attend the funeral of nephew.

Title of Book: *Julius Cæsar*
Author: *William Shakespeare*

Having completed the Reading and Study of the above book on (date) _____, I would like to make the following notes as a record:—

It is a story concerning *the death of Julius Cæsar and the struggle between his supporters and his murderers.*

The book describes *Cæsar's triumph in Rome and the forming of a plot to kill him. After Cæsar's death Brutus, Cassius & the others in the plot are beaten by Marc Antony and die under tragic circumstances.*

The most interesting part is where *the conspirators and Marc Antony are taking sides just after Cæsar's death. This is the tense point of the play.*

The character which appeals to me most is *Marcus Brutus* because *he seems to have noble ideas and not only to think of himself. He is brave and composed.*

The one I like least is _____ for in this case _____

Of the other characters I would mention:—
1. *Marc Antony*
2. *Cassius*
3. *Portia*
4. _____

Note.—If you dislike the book in any particular, make a note of same with reasons on the next page.

Mona Cunliffe, English work 1921

Mona Cunliffe Geography work

1922.
January 19th, Mrs Beaumont sent home at 11 a.m. owing to loss of voice.
February 1st Miss Ballantyne, the teacher appointed to commence duty in October in place of Mrs Curran, has not yet arrived.
April 26th Today two boys (Harry Mylchrest and Tom Eyres) accidentally broke a window with a golf ball. I have asked them to pay nine pennies each.
May 3rd. Today, Mr Walsh complained about Mr Etchells having hit his daughter (Edith) on the back with a cane.
May 19th. Mrs Rylance again absent this afternoon, owing to illness of baby. Two teachers short today.
May 29th. Attendance very poor. Several cases of scarlet fever and measles. Average last week, only 339, and today there are 40 children absent.
June 29th. Winifred Unsworth, a scholar has been awarded a five-year bursary by the Lancashire Education Committee.
July 10th. Mr A. Hudson, an ex-soldier in training at Erith, Kent, commenced a period of school practice.
July 24th. At the Ashton County Police Sports the school was again

successful in winning the first prize and victory cup in the half mile team race for schoolboys. 23 teams competed.

August 1st. Staff. John Tomasson. J.G Brayless. Miss Marion Walker. Miss M Lea. Miss E Park. Miss A E Murray. Mrs Rylance. Mrs Rush. Mrs Beaumont. Mr Etchells.

1923.

February 2nd. Mrs Rush late this morning. She has only been on time one morning this week.

February 14th. Lately, several parents have complained about personal remarks, having been made to their children by Mrs Rush. Mrs Talbot complained today. I spoke to Mrs Rush today concerning this.

March 13th. Miss Lea absent today. Permission given to visit a school at Leeds.

May 9th. Complaints have been received from parents (Mrs Flood, and Mrs Swindells), regarding Mr Barlow treatment of their daughters Vera Flood and Margaret Swindells. I spoke to Mr Barlow, concerning each of the complaints.

May 11th. Mr Strafford complained about Mr Barlow's attitude towards his daughter Florrie.

July 9th. Although I've previously spoken to Mr Barlow about the practice of allowing children to mark their own work (arithmetic). I had to point this out again today. The books are very unsatisfactory.

July 25th. Received a letter from Mr Knott saying that Mr Barlow had applied for leave of absence during the period of residence in a sanatorium for tuberculosis patients.

July 30th. At the Ashton County police sports the school was successful for the third successive time in winning the victory cup in the half mile team race for schoolboys. 20 schools competed.

August 1st. Mr Barlow on leave of absence.

October 8th. Miss Lea again absent, and Miss Park was so ill (following an operation), that she had to go home immediately. We are, therefore, again three teachers short, and without heat in the school. Under such conditions, satisfactory work is impossible -- 412 present in the afternoon, and only six teachers and myself to deal with them.

November 8th. Received letter from Mr Knott saying that he had received tender of resignation from Mr Ernest Barlow. He has been absent since July 17th.

November 21st. Mrs Acton complained about Mr Etchells. Her son is a very trying boy.

1924.

January 14th. Miss Park returned to duty. Absent three days.

February 22nd. Miss Thompson completed her engagement as temporary teacher, having taken an appointment at Gee Cross, Hyde.

February 25th. Mr Brayles, absent today. Influenza.

April 1st. Mr H L Shaw, commenced duty as certificated assistant in place of Mr Barlow (resigned).

June 3rd. In a writing competition open to schoolboys and promoted by Bradley's clothiers, Frank Evans gained first prize. Norman Dellow and Fred Jones, gained consolation prizes.

June 20th. Copy of the report of her Majesty's Inspector.

It is now about four years since the Headteacher was permanently appointed

to his present position, and has had time to make his influence felt, and to arrange settled schemes of work. In the matter of getting orderliness and attention in the classes, and in establishing a very consistent standard of neatness he has been successful, and his terminal reports show that he discerns and does not hesitate to point out weaknesses in the instruction. He has done a good deal towards replenishing the stock of books and materials, which had been allowed to run very low. These are important things and credit is due for the achievement, but there is a fundamental matter in which progress is less evident, and to which both he and his assistants should give their earnest attention. Each class appears at present, to be exclusively concerned with the work of the current term or year, and the relation of the task immediately on hand to the scheme of work as a whole usually receives too little attention. There is a clear need for better coordination of effort, and in order that this may be possible. It is necessary that all teachers should take measures to acquire a better knowledge of the scheme as a whole, and that they should give serious thought to the means by which they can best make use in their own class of knowledge that the children have gained in previous classes, and also in their own course render prominent the positive knowledge that will be necessary to progress at a later stage.
It is suggested that this may be best attempted through regular staff conferences, and the following matters -- of varying degrees of importance -- which arise during the course of the inspection might well be given a prominent place among the subjects thus brought under review.
The continuity and progression of the colour working drawing. The use of contour maps and other modern devices in the teaching of geography. The place that the study of literary forms, e.g., rhyme,rhythm and metre in verse, should have in the work of the upper classes. The best means of increasing the children's output in the composition exercises.

July 28th. At the county police sports, the school running team was successful in winning the cup given for the half mile schoolboy team race. This is the fourth successive victory. 19 schools competed.
September 1st. Mrs S. Foulkes commenced duty in place of Mrs Rylance who resigned.
December 9th. For some time, the attendance has been very unsatisfactory. This morning I questioned all yesterday's absentees, who are present today -- about 25. The answers given (minding the baby, going on errands, helping at home) show that there is much neglect and want of attention.
1925.
January 13th. Miss Park, absent today -- bad face.
March 31st. Today Mr Etchells concluded his career as a teacher. He has been on the staff of this and the old school for 47 years.
May 15th. Absent today -- severe body pains.
July 27th. At the county police sports school running team was again successful in winning the cup given for the half mile schoolboy team race. This is the fifth successive victory.
August 3rd. At the Droylsden sports, the boys running team was successful in winning first prize. The girls team also won first prize and the cup. The school now holds three silver cups for sports.
September 29th. Two accidents have happened in the yard today. This

morning, a small boy (F. Willis), trapped his finger with the back gate, and this afternoon Albert Hall fell in the yard and cut his eye.
November 4th. Mrs M. Doyle commenced temporary duty this afternoon in place of Mrs Woodall, who has been absent since September 22nd.

1926.
February 26th. Mrs Davies and Mrs Doyle, temporary teachers completed their engagements.
March 26th. On Friday afternoons several of the older boys are being allowed to dig up the garden soil. This is to be done after playtime.
May 4th. Miss Murray absent today owing to the difficulty of travelling due to the general industrial strike.
June 8th. Miss Park, absent this afternoon to visit an eye specialist.
June 28th. An oak shield, with bronze centre, has been presented to the school by an anonymous donor, to remain in evidence of the fact that the school netball team has, for two successive years, won the championships of the Ashton and district schools netball league.
July 26th. At the county police sports, the boys running team was again successful in winning the cup given for the half mile schoolboy team race.
November 2nd. Miss Winchester commenced duty as assistant mistress.
November 19th. Violate Owen trapped her finger with the wheelbarrow in the yard during playtime this morning. Miss Lea attended to her and she was afterwards allowed to go home.
December 21st. Yesterday I had occasion to speak to Mrs Rush, regarding a small irregularity. This afternoon, she is absent, probably partly due to worry.
1927.
January 17th. Mr Norman Higson, a student in training at Chester training college, commenced a week's school observation.
April 27th. Mr John Booth, commenced temporary duty.
June 3rd. Mrs Rush has been granted three months leave of absence, spending a holiday in America.
June 20th. Mrs Murray, absent this morning. Received a note saying that she had broken a blood vessel on the brain. We are now three regular teacher short, and the work is suffering in consequence.
July 18th. At the Droylsden sports, the boys running team was again successful in the half mile team race.
July 22nd. Allen Parkinson and Charles Frier had been awarded free admissions to the Openshaw Junior technical School.
July 25th. At the county police sports the boys running team was successful for the seventh successive time.
September 23rd. Geoffrey Stead, a former scholar, has been awarded a university scholarship of £75 per annum.
October 11th. Left school early this afternoon to attend the funeral of Mr Etchells -- a former teacher.
November 7th. Miss Alice Buckley commenced duty in place of Miss Murray (retired).

1928
February 27th. Mr Gleave, absent today. Unwell following vaccination.
March 12th. Miss Lea late this morning. Travelled from Doncaster -- 11:25

a.m. when she arrived at school.
May 17th. Ascension Day -- holiday in the afternoon.
May 24th. Empire Day -- holiday in the afternoon.
July 2nd.. extract from report of her Majesty's Inspector. The school is organised in nine classes. The tension is called to the wide age range in certain classes.... It is regarded as of increasing importance that all scholars of 11 years of age and over, should be provided with a three years course at the end of their school life, it is desirable that experiments should be made with a view to discovering appropriate exercises for the weaker children, and that the organisation should be reconsidered on these lines. Some retardation of scholars has been noted in the various classes. In December 1926 it was remarked that 58 scholars had been kept in the same class in which they had been working the previous year. The number of cases in which this had recurred in the current year had fallen to 17.... Though the working of the school may have been affected during the past year by absences of various members of the staff, it is pointed out that the school is very generously staffed as there are 10 teachers, including the headteacher for an average of attendance of about 300 scholars... Written exercises are for the most part, neatly done, but unequal results were seen in the exercises in written composition... In geography and history, except in standard seven, the children's knowledge of the matter of the lessons was vague and inaccurate. Generally the teaching should make a stronger appeal to the scholars interest.
July 30th. At the drawers and sports the school running team is successful in the half mile team race and won outright the Smith cup... School has now won 3 cups out right.

1929
January 21st. Today Sam Heath, who was disobedient last week was again disobedient to his teacher. His father, who did not come, was sent for, but at the request of his aunt, who came to school he was given one stroke on the hand.
March 28th. Miss E Park completed her engagement as assistant. She has given a long and faithful service.
April 19th. During gardening lesson, Herb Foreman was accidentally caught on the forehead by the spade of another boy. The bruise was not severe, but caused a cut about an inch long. He was sent home.
November 6th. Complaint made to today regarding Mr Lowes, treatment of Elizabeth Hallworth.

1930
February 24th. Mr Foulkes absent, by permission, today. Attending interview at Birmingham.
March 31st. End of financial year. Average attendance for year 299.9. Mr Foulkes is completed his engagement as assistant to take up an appointment at Barnes Homes Industrial School.
May 30th. Clifford Mortimer has been awarded a county junior scholarship, tenable at Ashton-under-lyne secondary school.
July 9th. Joan Haughton has been awarded a county scholarship at Fairfield High School for Girls.
September 1st. School reopened after a holiday.
September 30, Mrs Rush terminated her career as a teacher after serving on

the staff for more than 30 years.
1931.
January 15th. Mr Hitchin (Band of Hope Union) gave temperance lecture.
June 2nd. Dora Cretney has been awarded a County Junior Scholarship at Fairfield High School for Girls.
July 8th. Edith Ainsworth has been awarded a Junior Scholarship at Central High School, Whitworth Street.
August 31st. James Ireland and Mr Allen Young have been awarded junior art scholarships at Manchester School of Art.
November 11th. Armistice Day -- holiday in the afternoon. Special lessons on League of Nations and silence observed.
1932.
February 9th. Shrove Tuesday -- holiday in afternoon. Mrs Booth complained about Mr Lowes treatment of her daughter Irene.
February 29th. Today the strong wind blew the door to, and it trapped the finger of a girl Elizabeth Bray, causing damage of the nail. Miss Winchester attended to the girl.
April 4th. Receive notice that Frank Grimshaw had in the junior scholarship exam ,1932, reached a sufficiently high standard in the written examination to warrant his being considered for the award of a junior scholarship without an oral examination.
July 25th. Norman Wilson has been awarded a Junior Technical Exhibition, tenable at the Ashton-Under-Lyne Junior Technical School.
September 5th. Miss E Thorpe commenced duty as assistant mistress in place of Miss Winchester.
September 23rd. This morning while marching round the cloakroom, Edna Coppack fell and injured her finger. Miss Lea tended to the girl who was afterwards sent home.
1933.
March 24th. Mr Ball came to investigate the case of punishment given to George Hatlow by Mr Morley.
March 29. Today just before morning lines were called in a large alsatian dog ran in the yard and bit Fred Bowers, a boy in class D. The boy was immediately sent home, and I afterwards interviewed the owner and the boy's mother.
May 31st. William Broadley has been awarded a Junior Scholarship.
September 4th. Mr Greaves commenced duty today in place of Mr Lowe who resigned on August 31. The interior of the school has been decorated during the holiday.
1934.
January 31st. Miss M Kay left on this date to take up an appointment at Old Trafford. Miss E Thorpe left on this date to take up an appointment at Accrington.
February 16th. Received notice that Mrs Beaumont had claimed a breakdown allowance, and that her resignation was to take effect from January 31st.
July 17th. 154 children are absent this afternoon -- probably due in most cases to the visit of King George and Queen Mary to Manchester. Connie Hindle has been awarded a scholarship £10 per annum.
November 29th. School closed today to celebrate the marriage of Prince George and Princess Marina of Greece.

December 17th. Harry Furness has been awarded a handwriting prize in the competition promoted by the children's newspaper. The competition was open to all the schools of Great Britain.

1935.

April 10th. Robert Wilkinson has been awarded a Junior Technical Exhibition, tenable at the Newton Heath Technical School.

May 24th. Empire Day. Holiday in the afternoon.

May 30th. Ascension Day. Holiday in the afternoon.

May 31st. Harry Hodgkinson has been awarded a junior scholarship.

December 17th. Today in the presence of a woman who was making application for the admission of a boy, Miss Wilde caned two children (not severely). When I spoke to her concerning this Miss Wilde said that she did not know that the woman was present.

1936.

January 8th. The children gave a performance of Dick Whittington, to which parents and school managers were invited. The effort was very successful.

January 20th. A very bad wintry morning. The roads and paths were covered with wet melting snow, and travelling is very bad.

January 28th. School closed today. Funeral of King George V.

March 3rd. Ronald Adshaw fell in the yard and fractured his leg.

May 28th. Alan Firth and James Blakeborough have been awarded junior scholarships. Joan Summerskill has been awarded a Manchester scholarship.

November 27th. The weather has been very bad, the whole of the week -- fogs every day. In consequence, the attendance has suffered heavily. Average attendance for the week, 417. Number on books, 516.

December 3rd. Three teachers (Miss Nicholson, Miss Wilde, and Mr Morley) were involved in a bus accident today. Miss Nicholson arrived late due to suffering from frights. Mr Morley and Miss Wilde were taken to Ancoats Hospital for treatment -- Mr Morley has shock, and Miss Wilde cuts and bruises about the face. Mr Morley returned to school in the afternoon, but Miss Wilde had to go home.

1937.

February 17th. Ronald Hyde while playing in the yard this afternoon, caught his head on the wall and cut it rather badly. The school medical officer was in school at the time and gave every possible help.

May 11th. School closed today for Coronation and Whitsuntide vacation -- 1 week and four days. Coronation souvenir medals and pencils presented to the scholars on behalf of the Urban District Council.

July 15th. Copy of Her Majesty's Inspectors Report. There are 506 children on the books of the school organised into 11 classes. Two classes have to be accommodated in the assembly hall and crowded conditions have of late, disturbed to some extent, the orderly progress of the school. The headmaster has been here for many years, and he continues to conduct the school in a kindly manner. He is assisted by 11 teachers, all of whom work conscientiously, but with varying success.......... Responsibility should be delegated to one of the women members of staff in order that the special interests of the girls may be safeguarded. It is also essential that the inch corruption in needlework, should be properly coordinated and conducted in accordance with modern thoughts............

November 5th. School closed this afternoon on account of the Peace Pageant by the combined schools of Droylsden.

1938.

May 20th. Visit of the King and Queen to Ashton. To allow children an opportunity of seeing them the school will open this afternoon at 1 p.m.. 121 children absent in afternoon.

June 14th. Scholarships and exhibitions gained this year. Fred Redfern. Kenneth Ellis. Ronald Ellis. Eric Sanderson. Ronald Norcross. Eunice Davidson. Eunice Simpson.

July 14th. Eric Selby has been awarded a Hobson's scholarship.

September 26th. School closed this afternoon at 3:30 p.m., on account of the school wanted for the distribution of gas masks.

October 21st. This afternoon children 11 years of age and over attended a lecture in the Co-operative Hall on tuberculosis. The lecture was illustrated by films and lantern slides.

December 20th. Leonard Willis and Albert Broadley have been awarded exhibitions.

Year 6

Chapter 3   The war years   1939-1945

INFANTS
1939.

June 19th. Visited in the morning and found extreme disorder, owing to the forcible entry during the weekend by irresponsible person or persons.
December 14th. Arthur Moran slipped in the yard at playtime and broke his arm. His mother was sent for, and took him by car to Ancoats Hospital.
1940.
February 1st. Miss Summer returns this afternoon at 1:30 p.m. after being absent seven half days, snowbound. Her journey today from Wilpshire(?) took her 6 1/2 hours.
May 14th. On Saturday, the government broadcast a message that all schools in neutral areas should resume duties today. All the staff returned but only 220 children out of 300.
September 16th. We reopened school this morning owing to sirens being sounded as the children were on their way to school. It was 9:50 a.m. before we assembled. There were 210 children present, and all the staff.
1941.
May 14th. This afternoon, we take the children to the pictures to see a National Savings Film.
1942
September 15th. During play this afternoon, Peter Greener, aged five, fell and hurt his arm. His teacher took him home.

1943.
April 5th. This morning, Brian Oliver, age 6, swallowed a halfpenny. He was taken home by his elder brother from the upper department.
July 13th. During playtime this morning, Roy Haslem, aged 6, fell in the yard and broke his arm.
September 30th. Before resigning my position as headmistress of Manchester Rd Council infants School, Droylsden, I desire to pay tribute to my staff. A more loyal or conscientious set of teachers it would be impossible to find. Without their loyal support, the school could not have been carried on, as it has been. Annie Heys.
I, **Annie Heys**, retire from the profession today.
November 3rd. School reopened after mid-term holiday. **Miss A Rigby** began duty as headmistress of the school.

1944.
January 13th. Miss Evans of the wartime nursery called in the afternoon. Borrowed 12 plasticine boards and 12 children's blackboards for the duration of the war, with the authority of Miss Jones, and Miss Smith.
February 14th. Opened school at 9 a.m. for the first time during the spring term. As the milk was delivered late at 11:10 a.m., the order for the day was cancelled, as the milk would not be digested before dinnertime.
April 26th. Amanda Williams, aged five, was playing by the van for school dinners when the back door of the vans swung to close and the middle finger of the childs left hand was crushed at the top. The finger was dressed, and the child was taken home.
May 17th. Miss Oldfield, county organiser, visited in the afternoon, bringing 150 sandbags to be made into individual towels.
July 3rd. Salute to the soldier week. £283 was collected by the savings group.
July 13th. Brian Smith slipped on the wet surface of the yard and cut two fingers deeply on another child's magnifying glass. The wound was dressed and the child taken home.

1945.
January 22nd. Due to the strike at Bradford Road, Gasworks, the caterers were unable to deliver the midday meal punctually. The children began their meal at 3 p.m.
January 31st. The school was closed all day, due to the lavatory pipes being frozen, the toilets were in an unhygienic state. The staff stayed at school to supervise the midday meal activities.
March 12th. Began the collection of household articles to be sent to the bombed out families of Ilford.
October 24th. At 1 p.m. today, the meals van was being driven out of the back gate of the school, with the doors swinging open. One of the doors became wedged between the gatepost and the van. A crowbar had to be used to dislodge the van. This displaced the gate and brick gatepost, which are now in a dangerous position.
November 30th. **Miss A Rigby** resigned her post as headmistress of this department. She is to take up a similar appointment at Linaker Street School, Southport.
December 3rd. **Miss C.Tegg** commenced duty as headmistress of the school.
December 14th. Iris Johnson fell in the playground during the afternoon

break. She cut her knee and received first aid treatment from a member of staff.

Nathan Mcfetridge

JUNIORS 1939-1945

1939.
July 10th. Scholarship winners this year. Frances Stedman. Mary Wilshaw. Audrey Nicholl. Frank Maddison. Annie Holbrook. Albert Broadley. Leonard Willis. Cyril Manchester. Chas Sorenson. Harold Peers. Lawrence Green. Margaret Eleock. Dora Johnson.
August 2nd. Holiday this afternoon as a reward for scholarships gained during the year.
October 2nd. Owing to the outbreak of war the school did not open on the appointed date -- September 4th. It has remained closed until today. From today this call is being worked as a morning school and afternoon school -- half of each class attending each opening. The hours of working are to be 9 to 12 a.m. and 1 p.m. to 3 p.m. The two divisions will work alternate weeks.
1940.
February 2nd. Very bad wintry weather has continued throughout the week. The roads and paths have been thick with snow and travelling has been very bad. Many road and rail services have been suspended. The attendance is one of the worst on record. Average for the week 369 (69%).
May 31st. Miss E Jackson terminated her engagement as assistant mistress on this date. She takes up an appointment at Wigan.
June 19th. Scholarship winners this year.Roy Jones. John Stillow. Ivor Williams. Alan Marsland. David Pugh. Derek Goodwin. Bryan Trafford. Alfred Sewell. Cyril Dunnett. John Wilson. Geo Woad. Keith Ellerton. Fred Clarke. Kenneth Fletcher. Joan Perks. Joan White.Sylvia Frier. Stofton. Joyce James. Jean Baxter.Jean Skellen. Geo Ward.
August 29th. This morning 222 children are absent -- 308 present. Probably this is due to air raids on successive nights.
September 16th.From this date school will commence at 9:45 a.m. when an air raid has been in operation during the previous night between the hours of 10 p.m.and 7 a.m.
1941.
February 19th. Mr Greaves left to join the Royal Air Force.
May 7th. Today during afternoon playtime Derek Hibbert jumped on the back of another boy, Stanley Brocklehurst. Both boys fell backwards and Hibbert's collarbone was broken. Hibbert was sent home. Afterwards witnesses were questioned and the boy's father was interviewed, and he agreed that the injury was purely accidental.
May 9th. The attendance this week shows a considerable fall. Probably this is due to the nightly air raids, which have continued throughout the week.
June 27th. Scholarships for this year.Roy Greenwood. Ernest Vivien. Alan Voce. Harry Sutton. Rob Coulter. Kenneth Beard. Dorothy Mayfield. Florence S **thisellars**. Harry Baker. Frank Ratcliffe. Terence Murphy.
1942.
July 2nd. Scholarship winners this year.Stanley Crookall. Eric Knowles. David Bullen. Raymond Hilton. John Stalker. Reginald Sykes. Ernest Vivian. Derek Lomas. Elizabeth Oldham.
December 24th. School closed for Christmas vacation.
1943.
May 12th. Today Mr Allcock came to inquire about his son, Alan, aged 10 years of the having been struck on the head with a ruler by Miss Hallows. Mr Allcock pointed out that he was not complaining in any way about his son

being punished, but they preferred the punishment to be given in another way. In spite of the fact that Mr Allcock behaved as a perfect gentleman, Miss Hallows adopted a very wrong and unreasonable attitude, and as her manner became most unbearable I spoke rather strongly to her -- even in the presence of Mr Allcock.

May 21st. This week has been "Wings for Victory" week in Droylsden. The school raised £968 plus a £55 gift making a total of over £1024.

June 3rd. Ascension Day -- holiday in the afternoon. Marjorie Gray and Irene Jones have gained scholarships.

July 14th. Scholarship is awarded this year. Edwin Steadman. Geoffrey Crowther. Ronald Mather. George Edwards. Francis Howlett. Marjorie Gray. Irene Jones.

August 31st. Today I terminate my career as a teacher. Have been connected with the school (as scholar and teacher) for 55 years. Headteacher since June 1919. **John Thomasson**

September 1st. **Mr J. Gleave** commenced duties as Headmaster.

October 1st. School placed on 13 class organisation as follows. Mr Morley. Miss Lea. Miss Wilde. Mrs Ashton. Mrs Gillott. Mrs Nightingale. Miss Hallows. Mrs Payne. Mrs Hardy. Miss Brown. Mrs Whally. Mrs Duffy.

October 18th. Mrs Hardy absent. Husband on leave.

1944.

January 10th. School reopened after Christmas holidays. Number on roll 569.

January 14th. Scholarships. Peter Hutchings. Donald Johnson. Allan Timms. Marie Bevins. Alma Fryer.

February 22nd. Shrove Tuesday. School closed for afternoon session.

March 13th. Lecture on anti-person bombs and safety first by police.

May 12th. Army Sergeant Major visited each class in turn, to give 10 minute demonstrations, regarding the danger of grenades, etc.

September 25th. During playtime, Brian Clayton fell and fractured his leg.

September 29th. Keith Owen fell in yard during drill. No visible injuries. William Maddison hurt ear with a penknife in yard at 1:20 p.m.

October 19th. During lunchtime, the following girls -- Elizabeth Robb, Eileen Sutherland, Pat Stratfield, Joan Potts found £6 etc, hidden behind bowl in girls lavatory. Reported to and handed over to police. (The above affair was cleared up by the police).

1945.

July 17th. Senior girls visited reservoirs at Stalybridge in charge of Miss Lea and Mrs Nightingale. Left to score 1:40 p.m.. Returned 9 p.m.

November 12th. Mrs Hardy, absent. Husband on leave from Germany.

November 27th. Audrey Weaver fell during physical training. Injured mouth. Broke two teeth.

December 17th. Classes 9 to 13 inclusive, went to St Andrews in charge of their respective teachers to witness performance of the Emperor's New Clothes by the senior girls.

Sarah Hogan

Chapter 4 The post war years 1946-1960

INFANTS
1946.
April 17th. Jean Coley fell in the playground after bumping into another child, and cut her upper lip.
May 22nd. Ronald Lea was sent home to be taken to a doctor in order to remove a splinter from his finger received when picking up something from the floor of the classroom.
June 27th. Alan Shorrocks fell from his chair in his classroom. His arm was x-rayed at Ancoats hospital and the report said, that is probably a case of a fractured wrist.
December 13th. Joan Wilkinson collapsed during assembly. The parent was sent for, and Joan, along with Miss Duncan and the parent was taken to the doctors.
December 19th Miss Vernon, assistant mistress, retired from the profession. Miss Vernon has completed 38 years service in Manchester Rd School.

1940's

1947.

June 13th. Alan Cotton fell during his physical training lesson in the playground and cut his forehead.
September 26th. The harvest thanksgiving was held to which parents were invited. The gifts are being sent to Ancoats Hospital.
November 28th. The children had their royal wedding treats during the afternoon session. They had ices and games, and each child was given six pennies.
1948.

July 19th. The caretaker reported that the school premises had been broken into the previous day by two boys from the mixed Department of Manchester Rd School. The damage to the property was to the cloakroom ceiling, by which they had entered. The percussion band drums, and odd articles were taken, but all were recovered by the police. An attempt was made to set fire to paper in the hall.

October 19th. Mrs Clarke slipped whilst skipping with a child in a PT lesson taken in the playground. She received a knock on her nose from the child's head. Her nose was cut and her face badly bruised.

1949.

1940's

July 12th. Terence Allwood, slipped on the hall floor. Another child accidentally trod upon his arm, which sustained a break in two places below the elbow.

November 30th. A group of children visited the fire station in Manchester.

1950.

October 23rd. Miss M Hall was granted leave of absence, in order to attend a course for emergency trained teachers on clear thinking.

1951.

January 26th. Copy of Her Majesty Inspector's Report. This infant School occupies a substantial building in a site shared with the mixed school and is adjoining a busy thoroughfare. The premises include a hall and six classrooms. These give fairly satisfactory accommodation for the 224 children at present on roll. There are six classes and the hall is in constant use for the music, physical education and other purposes. Unfortunately the admissions in January, make it necessary for the hall to be commissioned as a classroom during the spring and summer terms, and consequently its value for the general school activities is reduced. In several other respects the premises are inadequate, washing-up after the midday meal, which is served in the hall has to be done in the cloakroom. Sanitary provision is poor and storage facilities, especially for physical education equipment are limited.

The headmistress was appointed in 1945. An energetic, enterprising and aware of recent practices in infant teaching, she directs the school in an efficient and pleasant manner. She has prepared helpful and progressive syllabuses, there is a well-balanced daily program and records were kept showing the progress of each child. In her own teaching, she sets a good example of skilful and sympathetic teaching of young children. There are seven assistant mistresses, five of whom are still comparatively inexperienced. All are sincere and hard-working teachers, who co-operate well with the head mistress in promoting the welfare of the children and give willingly of their time in the preparation of suitable apparatus and materials. There is a happy atmosphere in the school. The children friendly and confident in their teachers are given a good introduction to school life. They make excellent progress in reading, number and writing, and with the wealth of equipment the school offers they can find the opportunities for full development. At all stages they enjoy and profit by the various pursuits. The high standard of the social training is reflected in their natural yet orderly conduct in the classrooms and at the midday meal.

April 9th. The premises were entered by unauthorised persons during the weekend. The teachers table drawers were ransacked, but articles missing are trivial.

September 27th. Colin Ryden slipped when jumping during PT and fractured his arm.

October 10th. David Burrows slipped during PT. X-ray examination revealed a strained muscle of the elbow.

1952.

October 9th. A harvest festival thanksgiving service was held. The children's gifts were later taken to the Duchess of York Hospital, Burnage.

1953.
April 22nd. Mrs Mottershead attended a meeting to discuss Coronation celebrations for schoolchildren. It was decided that Manchester Rd School children should join St Stephen's children and attend a cinema to see a film of "A Queen is Crowned." They are to go on the morning of June the 16th and are to be taken in special buses from school.
May 21st. Mr Wild and members of the council paid a visit to this department this morning. They made a token distribution of pens (boys) and spoons (girls). The chairman spoke to the children and the National Anthem was sung. The school closes today for the Whitsuntide and Coronation holidays.
1954.
September 6th. **Mrs E Caitlich** started duties as head teacher.
September 27th. William Priestnall slipped in the schoolyard and cut his forehead.
December 9th. Two rodent officers came to school to deal with the mice in the classroom.
1955.
June 27th. A dog belonging to Alan Walker came into the playground at playtime this afternoon and bit John Bibby in class three on the leg. I reported the incident to police.
November 22nd. Lead flashing replaced on roof by county workmen.
1956.
June 4th. Members of the Birkenhead Youth Theatre company visited school this afternoon and gave an excellent performance of Pinocchio to all the children.
1957.
June 28th. The theatre youth players gave a performance of Hansel and Gretel to the whole school this afternoon
1958.
November 18th. Dr Bostock came to immunise 40 children against diphtheria.
1959.

March 4th. Graham Leighton and Paul Smythe were bitten by a stray dog at break this morning. The police were notified.

July 20th. Report by her Majesty's Inspectors. Since the last written report in 1950 the premises have been improved by the erection of a scullery for the school meals service and the installation of a hot water supply. The sanitary provision, however, remains unsatisfactory, the flooring in the hall, and in some other classrooms is badly worn and storage facilities, especially for physical education equipment, are extremely limited. Some suitable pictures from the classrooms and floor covering for the staff room, would improve the appearance of the premises, which, in general are well-kept, apart from the piano, which appears to have served its time and should be replaced, some old infant furniture in classrooms and some minor items that were discussed with the headmistress.

The headmistress, who was appointed in 1954 after seven years as headmistress of a small infant school elsewhere, is to be congratulated on her unobtrusive leadership of a staff of more than ordinary ability, and on her conduct of the school in general. She has so organised the school that it's been possible to discontinue using the overcrowded hall as a classroom, has prepared progressive schemes of work and planned a well-balanced daily program. The six assistant mistresses provide between them a nice balance of youth and experience. They co-operate well with the headmistress and, in addition to conscientious teaching, give readily of their time in the preparation of supplementary material and apparatus. Some of it is most ingenious... their work is informed by a knowledge of modern methods of infant teaching, and by a diligence, which is wholly commendable.

The children are given a sound introduction to school life in a happy atmosphere. Most of them make good progress in reading, writing and number, and those who find the acquisition of these skills difficult, receive special attention from the headmistress. The book corners in every room are well used, and an excellent selection of books is also displayed in the hall. This close attention to the provision of suitable reading material is followed up by a great variety of opportunities of self expression through speech, writing, art and craft. Music plays an important part in the curriculum. Most of the staff are pianists, several suitable broadcast programmes are regularly used, there is a percussion band, and the repertoire of hymns sung at the morning assembly is notable. The well-stocked nature tables, and the many other features designed to engage the interest arouses the curiosity of the children and are indicative of the quality of the all-round training that is given.

The natural and confident behaviour of the children in the classroom, at assembly, and at the school meal taken in the hall, reflects the quality of this training, and the esteem in which the school is held by the parents is evidenced by the extremely well attended open day. This is a very good infant School.

December 1st. The school was broken into during the night by some person or persons unknown. Entry was gained through a window in the kitchen. The place was left in the state of great disorder. Three windows were broken, the kitchen and staffroom doors were broken in, and cupboards and desk drawers all broken open and contents scattered about the floor. The national saving stamps and money (£10) were stolen. The caretaker had informed the police who were in school when I arrived at 7:55 a.m.

1960.
July 19th. This afternoon, one of the electric lights in room five crashed to the ground and the remaining flex caught fire. A fire extinguisher was used. Fortunately, the children had just left the room.

JUNIORS
1946.
April 4th. All seniors assembled at St Andrews Institute at 10 a.m. for cinematographic lecture on Africa and David Livingstone.
May 30th, Ascension Day. School closed at both sessions. (Mr Maxwell and five other teachers and 79 boys made a day tour of Castleton in Derbyshire).
June 28th. Bread projects completed and put up as exhibition today.
July 8th. Scholarships awarded. Clifford Pritchard. Neil Robinson. Roy Street. Peter Taylor. Seymour Borrell. Denis Lancaster. Shirley Bradbury. Sheila Brough. Gwyneth Jones. Josephine Jones. Barbara Shaw. Ann Williams. Norma Williams. Iris Barker. Lorna Cook. William Caveney.
December 6th. I wish to record the very meritorious work put in by Mr Crowden with the school choir. After much extra practice, the choir gave a concert in the large hall of Droylsden co-operative society. The hall was crowded, the choir sang well, and conducted themselves admirably, and the concert was an enormous success. Mr Crowden is to be congratulated on the results of his efforts.
1947.
February 28th. Mr G. Woodhall leaves today after 27 years as caretaker of these schools. He has been efficient, steady and always helpful. I am sorry that he is leaving.
March 17th. Accident to Eric Potts. Suspected broken arm.
June 18th. Timetable suspended from 2:15 p.m. All classes assembled on Lewis Road playing fields for inter house sports.
November 27th. Permission granted to choir to attend BBC audition 11:45 a.m.
November 28th. Wedding of her Royal Highness Princess Elizabeth. County shilling spent on sixpenny celebration and sixpence per child.
December 3rd. As a result of the BBC audition, the school choir has received word of their success and will feature in some future BBC programme. Mr Crowden is to be congratulated on the good work.
December 10th. The second annual concert was held at the cooperative all Droylsden, 7:30 p.m. The program was somewhat longer and more varied than last years and over 500 parents and friends attended and thoroughly enjoyed the performance.
1948.
June 14th. Report of Her Majesty's inspectors.
This large school of 692 pupils from seven to 15 years of age is organised in eight senior and nine junior classes. The latter six of which contain more than 50 children occupy the only classrooms at the main building. The first-year senior classes are in huts in the playground, for the last three years boys and girls are taught separately. The former occupy the school hall at the latter are in a parish hall, some 10 minutes distance from the main building. In either cases are their partitions or other means of obtaining privacy and quiet. The washing and sanitary accommodation is totally inadequate. As a result of

these conditions. It has been found difficult to get or keep staff, and since the appointment of the present headmaster in 1943. There have been 50 different assistant teachers. Of the present staff, eight are in their first year out of college and two others have taught for three years or less.

The work is further hampered by old-fashioned furniture and a deplorable shortage of equipment, particularly books. In spite of these limitations, the work in most classes reaches a reasonable standard and they can be said with confidence that both boys and girls are gaining from their extra year at school. A world planned projects has held the interest of the older boys, and has given opportunities for individual study. Both boys and girls have benefited from some interesting visits arranged in connection with their work. The older girls owed much to the influence of their senior mistress, but it is unfortunate that during the last few years they should be completely cut off from the life of the main school. Arithmetic in some senior classes should be more closely related to the children's needs and, for the girls, the time given to this subject might be reduced. Time given to English exercises might be devoted to more creative writing and to the study of literature, but it is difficult to cultivate a tasteful books, where there is no library, and few reading books of any kind. It is regrettable that biology does not form part of the senior girls curriculum. Religious instruction is taken conscientiously, but is hampered by the absence of Bibles. Instruction in handicraft is the responsibility of an enthusiastic probationer, who has the difficult but interesting task of the quip in his workshop making schemes of instruction and developing his teaching in close association with the main curriculum. Since the new workshop is used exclusively by this call, it is clearly necessary that it should be regarded as an integral part of the school and not as a detached centre administered independently. Only in this way can such integration be secured.

This is equally true of the new house craft hut, which forms a pleasant brightness in otherwise drab surroundings. The work is being done in both needlework and house Craft, but for the older girls, the latter needs planning on a more advanced level. The time allowed for needlework is too short to be of real value. The arrangements for the teaching of the subject will surely be necessary, and it is hoped that the longer periods can be given. At least one new sewing machine is required, preferably a treadle one.

The standards obtained in the junior classes vary considerably. It is pleasant to find few of the traditional oral lessons and more opportunity for the children to take an active part in their own education. It must however be emphasised that this approach calls for careful planning beforehand and recording afterwards, and the safeguards were not always apparent. In arithmetic that children should be led to discover more from themselves so that first-hand experience proceeds the manipulation of figures. There are few children who cannot read, at least mechanically, but again the work of all classes is hampered by the shortage of suitable books. Even so, more effort might be made to interest the children in good literature, both poetry and prose. In written English some interesting work is being done, but in certain cases this is marred by the lack of supervision. Too many children had difficulty in talking fluently about their work or other interests.

There is little in the surroundings to set the standard of good taste or aesthetic appreciation. This should be the special care of the headmaster and his staff. Suggestions were made as to how the morning assembly might become a more reverend and dignified occasion. Music can be a potent influence for good in the life of the school, and much interest and concern have been shown in the subject. It is essential that the musical training should be coordinated, that the scheme of work should show progressive development from the junior to the senior sections of the school and that the plan to be followed, should be supervised by the assistant master, who shows special aptitude and enthusiasm for the work. Boys and girls should, at all stages, be given opportunities for creative expression in art and craft. Shortage of material is hampering development in this field and, in one class, money collected for the school has been used to supply deficiencies.

The absence of free space indoors and the small playground, make it difficult to carry out a progressive scheme of physical training.

Throughout the school, there appear to be happy, relations between staff and children. The older boys and girls take their responsibilities seriously. The headmaster is to be congratulated on the good spirit, which has been obtained under very difficult circumstances.

1949
February 10th. Mr Smethurst absent. Influenza.
November 10th. Mr Jones sent home by order. Typhoid contact.

1950.
September 29th. 40 senior girls and 40 senior boys visited Droylsden library in connection with library centenary, from 3 to 4 p.m.
December 8th and 9th. Fifth annual school concert. For the first time concert held in school. Good audiences both evenings (240 on Friday. 210 Saturday.), the choir and orchestra gave of their best and Mr Crowden is to be congratulated on the result. Members of staff ably supported the occasion and the PTA social committee, catered admirably during interval.
December 15th. Exhibition in the evening of Christmas cakes etc.
Mr Williams 1950

1951.
February 28th. Mr Williams completed his service in this school, and takes over the headship of Duckworth County Primary School, Darwen.
April 3rd. 102 pupils over 13 years of age on first of September 1950, transferred to new secondary school, along with following staff: Mr Hargreaves, Mr Grace, Mr Johnson, Miss Richardson, Miss Wild, Miss Wilson, Mrs King and Mrs Curry.
August 18-25th. 249 children and 15 adults at Whiteacre.... Very successful venture.
September 4th. School reopened. 625 on the roll.
December 20th. Mr Crowden completed duty in this school to take up an appointment with Cheshire.
1952.
January 7th. School reopened. Burst boiler. No heat in main school. Junior classes sent home. Senior classes at St Andrews and Edge Lane, Methodists continued working.
February 13th. The announcement of death of King George VI.
February 14th. Violinists, under Mr Hough played hymns for assembly.
May 16th. Mr Lawton and class visited silk mill at Macclesfield, during afternoon session.
June 26th. Mr Richards and class visited Irlam Cooperative Margarine Factory and docks during afternoon session.
July 31st. School closed for summer vacation. All seniors to be transferred to do Droylsden secondary modern school. This school becomes a County Junior School. Mrs Howarth, Mr Lawton and Mr Foulds to go to new school, they completed their service in the school today.
September. Number of children on a roll 466. Staff. Headmaster, Mr Gleave. Mrs M Stait, Mrs V Yeaaland, Miss M Entwhistle, Mr R Beebe, Mr T Finn, Miss P Bailey, Mr J Wolfenden, Mr D Jones, Mrs J Scurfield, Miss M Hallows, Mr N Richards, Mr A Smethurst, Mr E Brewster.
The third-year boys will be accommodated in the prefab classrooms, and the third-year girls at St Andrew's Institute

1953.
May 20th. Coronation service in St Andrew's Church.
June 16th. School visited cinema at Guide Bridge to see Coronation film, as guests of Droylsden Council.
June 19th. 104 children, and over 10 teachers went on educational excursion to Liverpool and the Manchester Ship Canal.

SCHOOL CHOIR: *Teacher*—Mr. K. H. Gordon   VIOLIN CLASS: *Teacher*—Mr. L. Hough
Accompanist—Mr. J. A. Wolfenden

School Choir

1954 Football Team

SCHOOL CHOIR: *Teacher*—Mr. K. H. Gordon, M.A.   VIOLIN CLASS: *Teacher*—Mr. L. Hough
Accompanist—Mr. N. V. Richards, B.Sc.

1955.
May 13th. 150 pupils and 8 staff journeyed up the Manchester ship Canal to Liverpool and returned by train.
1950's School trip. Possibly to London

53

1956.
January 20th. Party of 130 children and parents visited Bellevue Circus for an evening performance.
April 1st. 39 children accompanied by Mr Brewster and Mr Millea left Droylsden to spend six days in London.
October 26th. Long list of prizes awarded to children for effort during the year.

I was at Manchester Road from 1949 to 1956. I remember some twit challenging me to a fight on my very first day. I ended up in Miss Tegg's office - ran home in tears. But after that it wasn't so bad. In the juniors who remembers the trip along the Manchester Ship Canal in the SS Egremont. We then went on the over head railway in Liverpool (now gone), and travelled home on the train. What a great day and all for 13/6!
Colin Ardron. (posted on our website)

1957.
March 1st. Six adults took 40 children to London for six days. A very instructive programme has been arranged.
September 6th. Telephone installed in heads room.
October 3rd. Report of Her Majesty's Inspectors. This all age school, which formerly occupied the site was reorganised in 1952 when the seniors were allocated to a new secondary modern school in the neighbourhood. An infants and a junior mixed school, each with a separate headteacher, remained on the site. The junior mixed school is attended by 456 pupils organised in 13 classes. Nine classes are in the main building, two in a hut in the playground and two in a parish hall some 10 minutes distance from the

school..... it must be said that the temporary accommodation in the parish hall is most unsatisfactory. The two classes held there have no partition between them, storage and display facilities are poor, cloakroom and sanitary provision is adequate and the hard playing space has an extremely rough loose surface.... in the main school. The playground is in need of repair, and the toilets for both boys and girls are without doors. The replacement of the old style dual desks by modern school furniture is proceeding slowly.... it is suggested that since all rooms are wired for broadcast programs. More use might be made of this aid. The supply of textbooks is adequate, but the stock of books in each class, which forms the class library consists mainly of old and obsolete works.... the staff consists of the headteacher and the 13 assistant teachers of whom nine are in their first appointment and four of these are in their first year of teaching. The staff of this school has been unstable for many years, there have been 18 changes since 1952. It is hoped that the present staff, some of the inexperienced members of which showed considerable promise, will remain unchanged. The headmaster has great concern for this school and has done much to engage the interest of the pupils and the support of the parents.... the children are friendly, and when their interest is aroused, very responsive. Many are keenly interested in their schoolwork and valuable habits of industry have been developed, particularly in the A forms..... much class teaching was seen and it is possible that the work in some classes is over, directed and here there is need for a much more individual work along the lines of the projects already developed in some classes. The teachers are conscientious and industrious and much thorough work is done on rather formal lines.... the morning assembly is reverently conducted by the headmaster and individual children read passages from the Scriptures. It was suggested that music on entry and at dismissal would add to the dignity of the occasion. The school meal, which is taken in the hall is most attractively presented under difficult conditions. There is an active parent teacher Association, which has done much for the school, including the presentation of the movable bookcases already mentioned..... the headmaster and his staff are to be congratulated on what is achieved in difficult circumstances. Improved accommodation and a much greater and better supply of books, with enlightened use of them, would do much to engage further the interests and abilities of the children.

1958.
October 30th. Long list of prizes to pupils.
1959.
January 27th. Maurice Pitcher fell in the yard at playtime. A broken right arm. Parents sent for and they took son to hospital by ambulance.
1960.
May 6th. School closed by royal edict on occasion of the wedding of Princess Margaret.

I was a pupil at both the infants and junior schools from 1958 to 1965. I then went to Littelmoss. I was in Mr. Beaumonts class for my top juniors. He was a great bloke, good story teller. Does anyone remember him making a cats whisker radio? Funnily enough many years later in 1991 I met him in Failsworth and we keep in touch. I have many happy memories of my time at Manchester Road.

Especially the two trips to Paris with Mr Davies. If you remember those trips, you might recall that on one of them Alan Roberts (later to be MP for Bootle) came while he was a student teacher. Those two holidays are still very fresh in my mind, even after nearly forty years. Eventually my son, Andrew came to Manchester Road 1980-87 and my daughter Claire started at Manchester Road in 1985. Hopefully the school will be there for many more generations to come. Good luck to you all.

Paul Lomas (posted on our website)

Sarah Hogan

Chapter 5   The sixties and beyond.
1961-1981

INFANTS
1961.
September 4th. The school reopened for autumn term. Could not admit new children owing to the flooded hall and classroom. The interior of the school has been redecorated during the vacation. The schoolyard is being resurfaced with tarmac. Outside of the school is being painted.
1962.
December 13th. Accident forms sent to DEO for William Dawson, who got splinters in his arm from the hall floor.
1963.
January 17th. The children were sent home and school was closed for the day as toilets were unusable owing to frosty weather.
1965.
September 27th. Today, taken as a holiday to celebrate the 700th anniversary of the Magna Carta and Simon De Montford's Parliament.
1966.
May 16th. School broken into by unknown person. Entrance gained by window in classroom. Pencils and biscuits taken. Police notified.
September 5th. New indoor toilets completed. New tile flooring put in all classrooms during summer holiday. Re-wiring of electrical work completed in every room.
November 21st. Fire discovered at 11.50am over entrance doorway into the kitchen. Caretaker applied fire extinguisher, fire service called. The fire was caused by a wooden beam, which was built into the heater boiler flue igniting from the heat. The fireman left about 2 p.m.
December 21st. **Mrs E Caitlich** terminated her services as head teacher on her retirement from the profession.
1967
January 9th. **Miss Ailsa Lawrence** started duties as head teacher.
June 15th. A special service was held today, World Children's Day. The older children dressed themselves as children from other lands and introduced themselves by saying a little about their country. Each class learnt a song, which traditionally belongs to another country. Three classes actually sang in French and one in Italian. The collection made to be sent to the Save the Children Fund.
October 17th. Last night again, the school was burgled. The thieves gained entrance through the windows in the roof and slid down the window cord. Caretaker has now sealed the windows.
October 18th. This afternoon we held a harvest festival. Each child had been asked to bring one piece of fruit, and it was presented during the service. We were able to invite parents of children in the oldest age range to come and join us.

Children 1967-68
1968.
April 4th. It appears there is a burst water main near school, so the water supply has been cut off. This has presented many difficulties including the need for washing hands and flushing toilets. A water cart was sent by dinner time to give water to flush the toilets.

1969.
January 7th. At 2:30 p.m the electric light fitting in room six exploded. The fragments fell to the floor, injuring David Barclay. A lump the size of an almond appeared on the top of his head. Mrs Richards, the class teacher bathed his head with a cold compress. As David was fretful, Mrs Richards took David home.
March 17th. During the weekend school was broken into. Three windows had been broken to gain access. The hall was in much disorder. Books thrown about.. Baskets of building blocks strewn around. Work on show was spoilt. Ornaments broken. Medical box rifled and items spoilt. Fire extinguisher used.
July 17th. The Adventure Players visited the school to perform the play, The Elephant Who Forgot.
December 15th. Stephen Rice tripped over the steps and fell into the rail on

the junior entrance door. He had a rather deep cut at the side of his face. I took him home and advised the mother to get the wound stitched.

1970.
June 1st. The school re-opened. An attempted break-in had been made during the holiday. Curtains had been fitted in the staff room.
September 1st. During the holiday work had begun on converting the outside toilets into a store room. Cupboards were built in room two and in the alcove. The partition in room two was put back making rooms two and three into one large room in readiness for our team teaching.
December 7th. The Theatre Players entertained us with their play, The Wishing Well. We invited the children from Bankside to join us.
1971.
May 17th. School was broken into during the weekend. Thieves ransacked the equipment stockroom and escaped via the toilet windows, which was pulled from the frame. The projector has been smashed.
December 20th. The Theatre Players visited school this afternoon and performed a play called Monkey Mischief.
1972.
January 28th. Letters have been sent out telling parents that school will be closed until further notice, because of the miners strike. Children will take readers home and asked to read a least two pages daily.
January 31st. The staff and school meal staff are attending school for normal school hours. Staff will spring clean cupboards, paint Wendy house furniture, repair books and make apparatus.
March 13th. School reopened.

1973.
June 14th. 170 children and 50 adults took the bus to Belle Vue to see the zoo park. The older boys have previously visited Salford Docks.
July 19th. At tea time, a passerby on the back lane, saw flames coming from the caretaker's store. Mrs Howard having remained on the premises, phoned the fire brigade, who came immediately and put the fire out. The store door had to be forced. The fire appears to have been started by the smoke from the incinerator chimney flaring on to the weatherboard and the roof was soon alight.
November 14th. School was closed, a compulsory closure for the occasion of Princess Anne's wedding.
1974.
March 5th. The police came to talk to the children about traffic lights, since they are due to be installed at the corner of Davenport Street and Manchester Road.
July 25th. Miss Phyllis Walstow, who joined the staff in September 1954, retires today.
1975.
February 17th. The exhibits we entered for the bulb competition were awarded first prize. The hall was decorated during half term.
June 10th. The first party of children accompanied by many mothers went by hired bus to Belle Vue to the Zoo Park during the morning.
December 10th. More than 50 children have entered the "sponsored matchbox" in aid of age concern in Droylsden. Certificates were awarded today.
1976.
July 1st. This past week has been very sunny. Milk is taken daily outside to the grassed area. Since it becomes excessively hot at dinner time, the children have the option of remaining indoors.
1977.
April 1st. Report of her Majesty's Inspector. With the exception of the lower reception class (35), all other classes have 38 children. Six teachers staff the six teaching groups. In addition, the deputy head utilises a separate room for withdrawal groups, children being taken from the top three classes of the upper school.... this is a good school, where work is soundly based on reading and number development. A long list of noticeably good features could be made, the following illustrate the most important ones. Behaviour and co-operation of pupils -- excellent. Social training and the giving of responsibility to children -- even the youngest. An air of quiet control in a "no bells" atmosphere..... responsible and caring attitude of staff.... music well covered. Good use of specialist talent, as well as individual teacher fortes. As indicated, the overall picture is one of an extremely good school.
One aspect of school-based education that was noticeably weak was the use of certain aids to teaching -- particularly TV and radio, and to a lesser extent projectors and cassette devices. We would in no way suggest that the curriculum is being seriously affected by this underuse more we are asking the question -- would thought for introduction and development of additional aids improve an already thriving educational environment? Also, staff need to review the storage of materials in classrooms. Can they suggest ways of increasing the amount of storage space without aggravating overcrowded

classrooms? Junior school liaison is still in its developmental stages, and although efforts to date are commendable, a more determined effort is needed if this vital area is to be fully developed. Staff of both schools are anxious to see this become more than an occasional cross transfer of pupils and teachers.

All the teachers are extremely hard-working. Their task is made difficult though by large class sizes -- and this would seem to be the real problem at this school.

May 23rd. Concert to celebrate the Queen's Silver Jubilee held this afternoon.

May 24th. A repeat performance of the Jubilee concert took place during the afternoon. The collection was taken in aid of the Mayors Jubilee Appeal. The sum of £24 was raised.

May 25th. Games were played in the yard during the early afternoon, and later the children went to the grass area behind school for a picnic tea. On returning to school, each child was presented with the Jubilee Crown in a case.

December 15th. Several parents accepted the offer to withdraw their children from school during the morning session, in order to see Prince Charles pass along Ashton Old Road.

1978.

November 13th. The Children Theatre performed The Story of the Red Ballet Shoes in our school hall.

1979.

February 16th. Staff again held up by difficult travelling conditions. Attendance was poor. At approximately 11.30 am there was a burst in the water pipes serving the kitchen. Water poured through the ceiling above. The dining-room assistants brushed the water out of the door. The Headteacher from the junior school climbed into the roof space and turned off the water.

1980

February 27th. A group of children were taken to the dairy farm at Mottram, by minibus.

December 3rd. Mrs Howard, an assistant to the school meals adviser has been monitoring the progress of a school meal from being cooked to arriving and being served in school. During the New Year parents are being invited into school at lunchtime to sample the school dinners. I repeated my complaint that the meal is lukewarm, and that would give parents concern.

1981

March. Copy of a letter from the Tameside Metropolitan Borough to all schools..... asking you to ensure that any school uniform regulations at your school were not discriminatory, but allowed female pupils to wear trousers in school uniform colours, if appropriate, where their religion requires this form of dress. I now realise that my original letter did not go far enough, since it related only to female pupils and not a female staff. It would also be discriminatory under the race relations act 1976 to ban the wearing of trousers by female staff, whose ethnic or national origins, mean that they belong to a religion which requires the wearing of trousers.

In addition, I have also taken legal advice, following a number of complaints on the question of discrimination in relation to other female staff, who are not permitted to wear trousers. This type of complaint would be considered under the sex discrimination act 1975. The general requirement for teachers to dress in such a way as to set an example of neatness and propriety to the pupils is no doubt justifiable, since it will assist in discipline, and in the enforcement of standards of dress and appearance among the children. Any general requirement would apply equally to both men and women teachers, and would therefore not be discriminatory. On the same basis, I can see nothing wrong with the ban on the wearing of jeans by both men and women teachers. However, trousers are nowadays an acceptable form of modern dress for women, and it would seem that a ban on trousers for women, could be discriminatory. An industrial tribunal may well uphold the complaint of sex discrimination by a female member of staff, who was disciplined for wearing trousers, which were neat and smart.

Obviously, the authorities are concerned to ensure that it complies with the law, both in its own actions and in the actions of its Headteachers, and under these circumstances, I should be pleased if you would ensure that all your female teachers and other female staff are aware that they are permitted to wear trousers to school.

Please ensure that all members of your staff are aware of the contents of this letter, and please arrange for the enclosed notice to be displayed in the school.

March 27th. The theatre players visited school during the morning to give a performance of the Wizard of Oz.

July 8th. City Councillors visited school to verify that the education committee had agreed to the amalgamation of the Infant and Junior School under one head.

July 14th. A luncheon was hailed as a social occasion to help integrate the staffs of the Infant and Junior schools.

July 22nd. A celebration afternoon was held in honour of the forthcoming wedding of Prince Charles to the Lady Diana. Parents and younger brothers and sisters were invited to join us the games, competitions and a party. The school managers presented the children with small china commemorative cups.

July 24th. School closed at 3:30 p.m. for the summer holiday. During the holiday, the central heating is to be refitted. When the school reopens in September. it will be the infant department of the primary school. The schools are being amalgamated. **Miss Lawrence** is to be the Headteacher for the joint school. Another page in history is written.

Kyle Lowe

JUNIORS

1961.
Programme for the Annual School Concert

THE NATIONAL ANTHEM

PART ONE

CHOIR

The Ballad Monger	*Martin*
Beauty Lately	*Handel*
Robinson Crusoe	*Folk Song*
Bonny Blue Handkercher	*Folk Song*
Cradle Song	*Mozart*
SOLO—RAYMOND CHARTER—How beautiful are the feet	*Handel*
The Frog and the Mouse	*Folk Song*
Sweet Nightingale	*Folk Song*
Three Crows	*Student Song*

VIOLINS

The Happy Wanderer	*Moller*
Springtide	*Woodhouse*
Sanctuary of the Heart	*Kettleby*
Clowns Dance	*Woodhouse*
Melodies by *Haydn*	*arr. Woodhouse*

INTERVAL

PART TWO

VIOLINS

Two Simple Pieces	*Woodhouse*
(a) Minuet	
(b) Valse	
Trepak (Russian Dance)	*Morand*
Rendez-Vous	*Aletter*
Finale from Beethoven's 5th Symphony	*arr. Woodhouse*

CHOIR

The Town Band	*Hunt*
The Gay Hunter	*Folk Song*
Rolling down to Rio	*German*
All through the Night	*Welsh Air*
Jesu, the very thought of Thee	*Wesley*
SOLO—RAYMOND CHARTER—The Crystal Spring	*Folk Song*
Chicadee	*Swedish*
The Mermaid	*Folk Song*
Oh dear what can the matter be	*Traditional*
Song for a Festival	*Dyson*

SCHOOL CHOIR   Teacher—Mr. J. WOLFENDEN
Susan Atherton, Sandra Barnes, John Blanksby, James Box
Janet Brackenbury, Michael Bradburn, Roy Bramhall
Erica Bridgeman, Irene Brindley, Enid Bromiley, Walter Brown
Margaret Burrows, Raymond Charter, Philip Coyle, Jean Craine
Hilary Doyle, Linda Egan, Audrey Everton, Edwina Fahey
Neil Fairhurst, Janice Finney, Christine Gilmore, Jacqueline Harris
Joyce Harrison, Janice Heald, Jacqueline Hamilton, Eileen Hardy
Lesley Heywood, Sandra Houfe, Georgina Hughes, Beryl Jenkins
David Kenworthy, Lesley Kirkland, Vivienne Lambie, Raymond Lee
Philip Lewis, Anthony McCarthy, William McCarthy
Patricia Maloney, Ann Massey, Barry Massey, Julie Mather
Valerie Nash, Susan O'Connell, William Ogden, Linda Parkes
Sylvia Payne, Valerie Pollard, Susan Power, Linda Roberts
Sheila Rooney, Hazel Ryan, Kevin Scott, Colin Seddon
Jean Stewart, Linda Stopforth, Dorothy Taylor, Paul Taylor
David Thompson, Barbara Williams.

VIOLINS   Teacher—Mr. L. HOUGH
Christine Barber, John Booth, Lesley Cavanagh, Christine Colvin
Joyce Duffy, Carol Melling, Christine Smith, Diana Windle
Lynda Dyer (Droylsden Girls' Sec. School), Margaret Lee
(Droylsden Girls' Secondary School), Beverley Dale (Fairfield
High School), Pamela Todd (Fairfield High School), Susan Smith
(Ashton Grammar School).

CELLO—William Ashton (Ashton Grammar)

PIANO—Mr. N. Richards

DRO 1017

Selby & Glover
OPHTHALMIC OPTICIANS

P. S. GLOVER, F.B.O.A.   M. GLOVER, F.B.O.A. (Hons.)
90 Gortoncross Street   393 Manchester Road
Manchester 18   Droylsden

Printed by F. H. & W. Greenup (T.U.), 62 Market Street, Droylsden

---

Droylsden
Manchester Road
County Primary School

Fourteenth Annual

CONCERT

Friday, 30th June, 1961

Programme Threepence

July 27th. Presented gold watch to Mr Woodhall (caretaker), who retires this holiday.
July 28th. Mrs Vernon completes her service today. She and her husband, the Rev Vernon are going as missionaries to South America. Mr Wolfenden, completes his service today. Both teachers have rendered valuable service to this school.
September 4. Staff. Mrs Street. Miss Taylor. Mrs Stait. Mrs Bird. Miss Hallows. Miss Bennett. Miss Horsman. Mr Finn. Mr Richards. Mrs Ainsworth. Mr Millea

1962
January 24th. Gaynor Almond, school prefect, in trying to liberate a kitten from a dog in the girls playground was bitten on the hands. Mother took her to Ancoats hospital.

1963.
April 5th. Today, Mr Alan Millea, completes his service in this school. I wish to record the loyal and devoted service he has given to this school, both in the school and also to the football teams which have had great success under his leadership.

1964.
February 24th. French evening for PTA. Explanation of methods by Mr Davies with illustration using children from standard one. This was followed

by playlets and songs in French by pupils from the second, third and fourth years.

March 20th. On Thursday, a party of 25 children and teachers leave for one week's holiday in Paris.

1965.

April 7th. Presentation to myself . I wish to record my sincere appreciation and admiration for the wonderful evening arranged by Mr Richards and staff and for the support of the PTA..... it is an evening I will always remember, mere words are inadequate to express my feelings and describe the evening and wonderful presents received.

April 9th. Today, I conclude my service in this school. After many happy years, feeling fully satisfied that Mr Richards my loyal deputy for 11 years, will carry on the established traditions. I would like to place on record my appreciation of Mr Richard's loyal and devoted service. The staff also deserve the highest possible credit who play their part in making this school a good name. **Mr Jas Gleave Headmaster 1943-1965.**

Manchester Road says 'goodbye, Mr Gleave

THE hall of Manchester Road School, Droylsden, was packed to capacity with parents and former scholars on Wednesday when a presentation was made to the headmaster, Mr J. Gleave, who is retiring today. There were even overflow gatherings in the classrooms off the hall!

Mr Richards, deputy head teacher, who will succeed Mr Gleave, said that the occasion was both happy and sad. Mr Gleave had first joined the staff of the school in 1926. In 1937 he took the post of headmaster of Haughton Green Church of England School and returned to take up the headmastership of Manchester Road School in 1943 on the retirement of Mr Thommason.

Councillor Mrs B. F. Wignall expressed the thanks of the Droylsden Primary School managers for the outstanding service of Mr Gleave for the children of Droylsden.

Mr Leslie Goddard of the Divisional Education Office staff, said that he had had a long association with Mr Gleave. There were times when he had fallen out with him but there were other occasions when Mr Gleave called him by his Christian name—(Laughter).

Presenting a cheque for over £80, which has been donated by scholars past and present, parents and friends, the Chairman of Droylsden Council (Councillor G. Seddon) said he had expected to see a sea of children's faces in the hall but instead he saw the hall was filled almost entirely with adults. That was a measure of the esteem in which Mr Gleave was held.

Mr Gleave, replying said that many mysterious things had been happening during the past few weeks. The old log books had vanished and there were meetings of teachers which broke up suddenly when he joined them. He realised that something was afoot. He thanked the donors of the retirement gifts.

A tape recording had been made of the ceremony and he would be able to play it back and listen to the voices of the school choir and the sound of the violins which would remind him of the long and happy days he had spent at the school.

AMBITION TO BE HEADMASTER

When he first joined the school staff as an assistant master it had been an ambition to become headmaster of the school. When the opportunity presented itself he was glad to take it. There had always been something special about the children of Droylsden for him.

Past scholars had become doctors, veterinary surgeons, and hosts of teachers, and the former captain of the England Rugby team, Eric Evans, was once a pupil. More recently a former Manchester Road School boy, now at the Audenshaw Grammar School, had been chosen to play in the English Schools Rugby side to meet Wales.

There had been many changes at the school during his years as headmaster. There were the teacher shortages of the 1940s when for three months he struggled to teach 120 children on his own. He had seen the introduction of the school choir and the class and the recent commencement of teaching French in the primary (which was pioneered Manchester Road).

Mr Gleave was also presented with a travelling and Thermos flask from school cleaning staff travelling case and clock the teaching staff.

Newspaper cutting

67

April 26th. **Mr N. Richards** commenced duty as headmaster. Mr Beaumont began his service in this school is deputy head.

1966.

July 5th. 50 children from the fourth year visited the safety exhibition at the armoury in Ashton.

November 7th. From today, we are allowed to use part of the playing field of Droylsden girls secondary school. Normally we shall use it Wednesday and Friday afternoon, for one hour on each occasion.

1967.

February 2nd. Staff meeting at 1 p.m.. Agreed to that children should not leave school premises at dinnertime (if they remain to school dinners), unless parents give consent in writing.

July 27th. Believers visit to Speke airport, New Brighton, the Mersey Ferry and Liverpool docks.

October 12th. Break-in at this school 4 panes of glass broken and money taken from various classrooms. The police spent the morning in school, taking photos etc.

October 18th. There was another break-in and the hamster in cage was stolen from the extensions staffroom. There is no insurance available through the office for school property

1969.

March 19th. Took 63 children on an educational visit to Belle Vue zoo.

April 30th. 4M visited the Stalybridge Waterworks and found it a stimulating experience.

July 23rd. Half day visit to Pilkington's.

1970.

February 20th. Monthly staff meeting.

July 21st. The school closed for the fourth year visit to Pilkington's Glass Museum.

November 23rd. Mrs Williamson's class went to Levenshulme to see the Express Dairies in connection with their schoolwork.

1972.

February 22nd. Children stayed at home in the morning due to power cuts.

June 19th. Third-year visit to Ordsall Hall museum Salford.

September 5th. Staff. Mr N. Richards, headmaster. Mr Beaumont. Mr Wellington. Mr Frank Blease. Mrs Pugh. Mrs Bird. Mrs Walker. Mrs Todd. Mr Carroll. Mrs Cole. Mrs Stait. Mrs Hudson. Miss Willetts. Miss Hallows.

	Sports Day Programme of Events Tuesday, July 11th				
1.	60 yards dash	1st Year Boys	11.	50 yards skipping	3rd Year Girls
	1st..........2nd..........3rd..........			1st..........2nd..........3rd..........	
2.	60 yards dash	1st Year Girls	12.	80 yards skipping	4th Year Girls
	1st..........2nd..........3rd..........			1st..........2nd..........3rd..........	
3.	60 yards dash	2nd Year Boys	13.	Potato race	1st Year Boys
	1st..........2nd..........3rd..........			1st..........2nd..........3rd..........	
4.	60 yards dash	2nd Year Girls	14.	Potato race	2nd Year Boys
	1st..........2nd..........3rd..........			1st..........2nd..........3rd..........	
5.	80 yards dash	3rd Year Boys	15.	Potato race	3rd Year Boys
	1st..........2nd..........3rd..........			1st..........2nd..........3rd..........	
6.	80 yards dash	3rd Year Girls	16.	Potato race	4th Year Boys
	1st..........2nd..........3rd..........			1st..........2nd..........3rd..........	
7.	80 yards dash	4th Year Boys	17.	60 yards egg and spoon race	1st Year Girls
	1st..........2nd..........3rd..........			1st..........2nd..........3rd..........	
8.	80 yards dash	4th Year Girls	18.	60 yards egg and spoon race	2nd Year Girls
	1st..........2nd..........3rd..........			1st..........2nd..........3rd..........	
9.	50 yards skipping	1st Year Girls	19.	80 yards egg and spoon race	3rd Year Girls
	1st..........2nd..........3rd..........			1st..........2nd..........3rd..........	
10.	60 yards skipping	2nd Year Girls	20.	80 yards egg and spoon race	4th Year Girls
	1st..........2nd..........3rd..........			1st..........2nd..........3rd..........	

Sports Day Programme. Price 1 pence.
1974.
January 10th. Mrs Svobada commenced to give violin tuition -- 3 hours each Thursday morning.
July 8th. Chester visit.
July 19th. Mrs Pugh returned. Absent for 1 1/2 day's. Her fainting fit was probably due to a practice shot with the starting pistol.
September 27th. 4th years went to the Hartshead Field Centre.
October 21st. All the lead was ripped from the roof on Monday night. This led to flooded classrooms and two classes working in the hall till roof repairs were affected. Later the whole of the hall floor rose and had to be stripped. The staff wrote a letter to the managers asking for steps to be taken to control vandalism.
November 18th. Fire and bomb drill at 2 p.m.
1975.
May 12th. The second year visited the Manchester Museum on the Oxford Road.
July 22nd. **Mr Richards** presentation took place in the afternoon in the hall. The children sang a selection of songs chosen specially from Mr Richards. Then Mr Graves presented Mr Richards with his leaving presents.
July 23rd. Babes in the wood was presented by the drama group to the rest of the school.
September 2nd. School reopened with **Mr Beaumont, acting head.**
wonderful to see that some of the first class teachers that we had, had been there for a long time. My best teacher was Mr Beaumont, who used to send one of our class into the butchers on the way back from the baths for some tripe. I was always terrified of my 'times tables' recitals at the front of the class-and the way he would throw the board rubber or chalk at anyone who talked during lessons!!!I also remember the free milk we had and how Mr Beaumont showed

us how to make butter from the cream off the top of the milk one day. The school plays(George & the Dragon etc)Choir practise and how Mrs Pugh used to patrol the choir making sure everyone was singing(and not miming!)I loved the hymms we'd sing at assembly(with the overhead projector) and how the worst punishment in the world was to be made to 'stand on the line'......oh I could go on and on....but if anyone wants to swap memories please get in touch!!!!
Brill Site!!
Joanne Rothwell (posted on our website)

1976.
January 5th. I, **Alan Beckett Smith,** took over as head teacher of this school. I record my appreciation of **Mr Beaumont's** successful endeavours as acting head for one term, to maintain the even tenor of the school's daily life. A full staff was present, and I met the school caretaker. Mr Beaumont attended to the orderly and organised entrance into the assembly hall. He also conducted the assembly to give me an idea of the format adapted. I spoke to the children at the end of the assembly and was pleased with the thoughtful responses to my topical questions. The Droylsden Reporter called in to ask the information about myself and my plans for the school.
January 7th. At a staff meeting, I stated my views on corporal punishment, namely that I hope it will eventually be phased out. At the same time, I would not deny a teacher the right to dispense summary justice by means of a smack if the offender failed to respond to reason. However, I stress that weapons such as rulers must not be used and that I would not excuse blows to the head under any circumstances.
January 16th. I spent much of Friday afternoon searching for a child who ran home after being reprimanded for spitting. His mother phoned in rather belatedly, at 3:30 p.m. to say he was with her.
February 10th. Contacted police regarding break-in during weekend.
May 18th. The new boy started today of Swiss parentage. He is just 12 years of age and officially of secondary age. However, we shall endeavour to teach him sufficient English to stand him in good stead when he moves on.
October 13th. 96 year four children, plus teachers went on a chartered train to London. We had an excellent outing and the weather was most kind. The children were extremely well-behaved and thoroughly enjoyed themselves.

I went to Manchester Road from 1971-78 and remember teachers such as Mrs. Walstow, from the infants and in the juniors I had Miss Walker who left to be replaced by the head masters wife Mrs. Richards. Before the end of the first year she was replaced by Miss Martin. In the second year I had Mr. Beaumont who nick-named me Tug, a name I am still known as today. In the third year it was over to the pre-fabs with Mr. Pickford and the fourth year I had Mrs. Ludlow. Good Days. I remember trips to London and Trentham Gardens on double decker Maynes buses with the headmaster Mr. Smith who use to sing 'in the quarter-master's store'. I remember when the lads use to recreate the scenes from the old Kippax and Stretford end stands in the shelter with the scarves and flags flying and every body use to get in trouble for acting like football hooligans.
Paul Gilmore (posted on our website)

1977.
March 3rd. A representative gave a demonstration of a photocopier to all staff. The teachers were not too impressed and felt that they would rather spend money on books.

March 23rd. Mrs Farrell's class visited the Opera House to see a performance of Winnie the Pooh.

April 1st. The party of 45 children left for a school holiday in the Isle of Man.

July 5th. We held a sports day on the Manor Road, playing field. The weather was excellent... we provided the children with ice cream during an interval.

October 19th. A party of 80 top juniors took part in an outing to London. 11 Tameside schools took part.

Julie White holds the rose bowl which Manchester Road School won in the Tameside bulb competition. With her is N

Winning the bulb competition 1978

School's bloomin' success

THE FOURTH annual Tameside Infant Schools' Bulb competition has been won by Manchester Road School, Droylsden.

Described by competition organiser Mr Alan Wright as superb, Manchester Road's entry comprised of a selection of various blooms, chosen both for their fragrance and beauty.

The competition attracted a record number of 45 entries, with over 6,500 bulbs being grown in the Tameside area.

The hyacinths, daffodils and crocuses were planted and looked after by the children, either in school or at home.

Planting took place in November, in bulb fibre provided by Tameside parks department and fortnightly bulletins were issued, giving tips and suggestions for better blooms.

Judging was carried out by Mr J. Sher, field recorder at the Hartshead Field Centre, who reported that the competition had reached a higher standard than ever before.

The prize for the winning school was a rose bowl, which was handed over by Mr Wright at a special presentation at the school on Friday afternoon. FEB. 1978

1978
May 23rd. The second year children went on the barge trip along the Ashton Canal.
May 25th. Staff meeting at 12:45 p.m.
June 28th. A psychologist called to explain to me and Mrs Pugh the causes of school phobia.
July 25th. In the afternoon we had a farewell ceremony for Mrs Stait, who is retiring after 33 years teaching in this school. After the ceremony a buffet was held and photographers from the Manchester Evening News and Droylsden Reporter took photographs of the occasion.
October 4th. I took a panel of four children to Droylsden library to take part in a Wombles Quiz.
October 18th. The fourth years went to London by charter train.
November 17th. This week seems to have brought about some change in the weather. We have had a phenomenal autumn, with temperatures in mid-

November being similar to average May temperatures. There has been little rain, which has led to a talk of draw out, especially in the southwest, and we have had some lovely, clear skies and warm sunshine..... a truly remarkable season, and one which gives credence to the suggestion that the seasons are changing!

1979.
April 6th. Took 49 children on a weeks holiday to Cullercoats, Northumbria.
July 19th. The third-year children visited Tatton Park and the fourth-year children visited Castleton.
July 26th. In the afternoon, a retirement ceremony was held for this Hallows, who has taught at the school for 37 years. In the morning, Mr Selby, the retiring caretaker after 18 years service, was presented with gifts.
October 17th. The trip to London was cancelled due to a proposed rail strike. I arranged a very last-minute outing to Castleton, which was greatly enjoyed by the children.
December 18th. Mrs Dorothea Bird, retired after 20 years in this school... an invaluable member of staff and one who will be greatly missed.

1980.
February 1st. Dinner money collected today at the new rate of 35p per day.
February 18th. The Young Ornithologists Club visited Martin Mere.
October 7th. The third years went to Chadkirk farm trail and the Ethererow Country Park.
October 15th. Visit to London with third and fourth years.
November 14th. A disastrous week with poor weather and staff absences. I have taught all week and have found it very wearing with all the other pressures. Today has been dreadful! It has rained non-stop, and the children have not played out at all.... wet dinner hours are a nightmare.

1981
January 12th. In the evening, six children attended Belle Vue Circus, as guests of Ashton Round Table.
March 9th. Governors meeting held in the evening. The decision of the Tameside Council to abolish corporal punishment in primary schools was discussed. The governors were unanimous in expressing concern at the decision and wish to know of proposed deterrents to replace the corporal act.
June 29th. Governors meeting. I announced that we had at last, a noticeboard affixed to the wall of the school alongside Manchester Road. It has taken more than seven years to achieve this result.
July 23rd. In the afternoon a ceremony was held to mark my farewell from this school. The authority has decided to amalgamate most infant and Junior schools into one primary school with one headteacher. It has been decided that I be redeployed as headteacher of Greenside Primary School from the first of September, and Miss Lawrence become head of these two schools, which will presumably be called Manchester Road Primary School.
July 24th. This closes my 5 2/3 years in office as head of this school. I've been extremely happy and I couldn't have had better staff, parents and children to work with. This book bears testament to the fact there had been problems, but my main memories are happy ones. I look forward to the challenge of my new post and wish my good friend, **Miss Lawrence**, a smooth merger and a successful time as the head of the primary school.
Alan Beckett Smith.

Memories of my time at Manchester Road

My name was Carol Smith and I attended Manchester Road School between 1975 and 1982 along with my older sister Janet Smith and twin sister Julie Smith. I have many happy memories of my time at school – I wonder if any of these recollections mean anything to anyone else?

I expect people will recall the headmaster, Mr Smith (grey beard), and his clapped out VW. Mr Smith would drive a small group of us to the music centre near Ashton. I was taught how to play the violin very badly. I recall one day, when we arrived back at school, the sliding door fell off the van!

I remember being the mouse monitor in Mr Beaumont's 3rd year class. I would take the mice home during the school holidays. I once had to wear an eye patch for a few days as a mouse had scratched my eye – I can't imagine how it happened. Whilst I was a mouse monitor, Julie was a fish monitor for Mr Pickford (Jolly Green Giant) and cleaned out the fish tank in the school hall with Samantha Bailey.

Probably, my best year in school with most memories was in the 3rd year juniors. Mr Beaumont was something different. He taught us how to gut a fish, skin a rabbit and make butter. We would have bingo number quizzes where we would have to stand on our chairs if we got an answer wrong and then on the table!! Don't think it would be allowed now.

Mr Beaumont made me a flute from a piece of grey pipe. I still have it and can still get a note out of it! Apparently Mr B used to make these flutes for the whole class in previous years.

I remember making table mats with willow and raffia. I was given the privileged role of handing out the raffia which would be hung at the side of the blackboard. Blackboards too – you don't see these in classrooms anymore. I remember them all being upgraded whilst I was at school from the static board on the wall, to a board that could be rotated.

I remember the sports days held out on Water Lane field – there are houses on there now. Also, in 1977 for the Queen's Silver Jubilee, I recall a school picnic on the field in the scorching sun. My mum had knitted me and my sisters red, white and blue jumpers with crowns all round!

Thinking of jumpers, I remember spending most of my school life wearing a jumper with my name written across the front! School uniforms can only be a good thing.

Mrs Pugh (drove a red Datsun Cherry) taught us all how to sing in tune. When she retired, Mrs Hudson who did most of the music, wrote a song, 'Oh Mrs Pugh, What shall we do? Our singing just won't be the same here without you! This funny feeling, keeps round us stealing, Oh won't you throw retirement over do?...You make us Laaaa, and Paaaa each Tuesday, no exception, then practice, practice, practice 'til we're singing to perfection....' Why do I remember that song? Also, there was the song Milk Bottle Tops and Paper Bags. Does anyone else remember that?

I remember a school holiday to Gorebridge in Scotland with Mr Blease (and his family and Miss Trill). We slept in dorms like army barracks – girls in one dorm; boys in the other – with a linking door that caused all sorts of problems. Fun times!

I remember being taught how to play the recorder by Mrs Hudson. My sisters both played really well but I never really got the hang of it I suppose. I remember a Christmas concert when this was confirmed to me as I was moved off a recorder onto the Indian bells!

I remember Fanny Hallows. She did sewing with us when we were in 1st year juniors. I remember she made me stand on the carpet area in Mrs Farrell's classroom for flirting a rubber across the room with a ruler.

That was something else – Mrs Farrell's carpet. This carpet was a luxury and no other classroom had one in the juniors. The carpet was there because Mrs Farrell's classroom housed the library shelves down one wall.

I recall the prestigious move when the teacher thought your writing was neat enough that you were allowed to ditch the pencil and move onto a pen! We had to write with a forward slant and even though I did not find this natural, I remember having to re-do a whole piece of work for Mr Blease because my writing did not slant forwards!

School dinners – they were an education in themselves. We would line up and be counted in by the dinner ladies. When they had counted enough to fill a table, the next person would 'get the chop!' There was the pink custard in silver tank things that would be tipped down the outside grid if there was any left over. One day, Julie ran into the dinner lady carrying the dregs of the pink custard and it was all tipped over her head. The junior school kitchen had never had so many interested people while we watched the dinner ladies comb all the custard out of Julie's hair.

Other memories that I won't go into include:

School milk
Skittleball
YOC and trips to Martin Mere and Slimbridge with Mr Pickford
Singing the Lord's Prayer
Handstands against the walls
Having boys in one playground and girls in the other
Getting the cane or the ruler (although I never had it)
Skidders on the ice when it snowed
Playing in the playground shelters
Trips to London by train

I had a wonderful time at Manchester Road school and made many friends – many of whom I keep touch with now.

Thanks
Carol Moxon (Smith)

Chapter 6 The last decades of the century. 1981-1999

1981.
September 1st. A new phase has begun in the life of this school, which opened in 1907 as an all age school. During 1952, the seniors were all transferred to Droylsden secondary modern school, and this building became the junior school. From first of September 1981. The junior school amalgamated with the infant School on the adjacent site. I , Miss Ailsa Lawrence was appointed head teacher of the joint schools and the previous headteacher of the junior school was transferred to Greenside Lane Primary School. The staff is as follows;

Headteacher Miss Ailsa Lawrence
 Mr A Beaumont
Mrs M Pugh
Mrs C Hudson
Mr A Pickford
Mr F Blease
Mrs K Jewell
Mrs K Barnacott
Mrs J Naughton
Mrs C Page
Mrs B Banks
Mrs J Warburton
Mrs M Knight

Miss C Trill
Mrs S schofield
Mrs C ??
Mrs V Moore
Mrs J Lomas
Mrs J Saxon
Mrs P Ash

October 16th. Miss Lawrence was asked to award each child who had made a scrapbook about the Royal Wedding with a commemorative spoon.

1982
February 15th. Mr Pickford took the party of ornithologists to Martin Mere, the wildfowl trust, during half term.
March 9th. Mr Pickford and his class has spent the day at Compstall.
May 24th. The young Labrador dog came into the school yard. Six children were either clawed or bitten. All were sent home for parents to check that their tetanus immunity was still valid. The police were informed. The owner of the dog has apologised for the trouble caused by her dog and has contacted all parents concerned.
June 22nd. Mrs Brown in charge of the animal units at Longendale brought various farm animals to school (goat, sheep, rabbits, and even a Shetland pony).

1983.
February 3rd. Nurse Hollinshead told the cleanliness inspection. Mrs Banks and Mrs Barnacott took a group of older children to the ballet.
March 18th. Mrs Banks took her class to the Longendale animal units. Mrs Naughton and Mrs Barnacott took their classes to puppets galore at the Forum in Romilly.
April 28th. A special concert was performed by the children to thank Miss Madeleine Knight for her loyal service since fourth of June 1964.
October 7th. Mr Pickford and Miss Wells have taken their classes to Jodrell Bank and Ringway Airport.

1984.
February 17th. The school was broken into during the weekend, and every day the following week. Stock rooms were ransacked and many articles, including the Jubilee picture of the Queen were ruined. Many of the staff spent at least one day in school clearing up the building.
July 20th. The leavers gave an assembly. Miss Trill was presented with a basket of flowers and a cheque. She has worked in the school for 21 years without an absence. she is to work full-time at Greenside Lane primary School.
October 16th. A party of 60 children were taken to London for the day.

1985.
March 7th. Mrs Owen took a group of 72 children and five adults to see Charlie and the Chocolate Factory at the Liverpool Empire.
July 25th. A presentation party was held for Mr Alan Beaumont. He had been

deputy head of the junior school for 20 years. He retired because of poor health.
October 10th. Mrs Brown bought a selection of live farm animals to school. The goat was milked, and we had an opportunity to taste her milk.

1986.
June 27th. The chiropodist came to inspect the feet of children in year five.
July 17th. The seventh year children were taken to Romilly, Marple and Compstall via the canal towpath. This is termed the leavers hike. We left school at 10 a.m. and returned for 3:30 p.m..
July 23rd. The Royal wedding of Prince Andrew to Sarah Ferguson took place today. The children were able to watch the parades and weddings on the televisions. Each child was presented with a small cup keepsake by one of the year seven girls (dressed as a bridesmaid). Staff were given a commemorative spoon.
August 3rd. I visited school to discuss arrangements regarding the dry rot, and the heating repairs. My resignation takes effect on the 31st of August 1986, signed **Ailsa Lawrence.**
September 1st. **Mr John Bromley** took appointment as head teacher on this date.
October 7th. Staff meeting. Mr Bromley discusses philosophy and organisation.

1987.
February 2nd. Water penetrating school roof again -- over junior hall. Workmen discovers that large quantities of slates have been removed by youths to make gains dens on the roof.
February 16th. Extensive work on dry rot areas in infant and junior buildings.

1988.
February 16th. Environmental health visits -- the lead monitoring equipment is to be set up again in the school library -- will test levels of lead in the air on Manchester Road.
February 18th. Mr Alan Beaumont, ex deputy-head, visits to give talk on pigeon fancying to junior classes.
March 21st. Staff meeting, Mrs Barnacott leads on the teaching of spelling -- brilliantly clear exposition! Sheer professionalism.
September 1st. New teaching staff.Miss Tracey Hellewell. Miss Sara May. Mrs Christine Reilly.

I attended Manchester Road from 1981-1988. Now I am back working at the school, my memories seem to be merging past into present but I've written some of the memories I have.

I remember small milk bottles with silver tops and the blue straws. How I looked forward to break times, but not when the milk had been left out and it was warm! Also, there was once an assembly I was in with a Jamaican theme. I was dressed as a bird and I remember running up and down the hall singing *'Papa you see nobody pass here? No me friend'*. The second line involved something to do with dumplings!!! The mind boggles! We also got to watch Prince Andrew's wedding on the T.V.

One vivid memory I have is Mrs. Ellis scaring some of the last year juniors one dinnertime. We were having our Rubella injection and she said the needle was really big. I was scarred for life in more ways than one! The good thing is I can still remind her of this today as she's still at school!

So, from two head teachers – Miss Lawrence and Mr. Bromley, my first Reception teacher, Mrs. Schofield – whom I have been reunited with, the many trips – Jodrell Bank, Maritime Museum, making a needlecraft pencil case – which I still have and doing French in the last year, I have many happy memories at this school which is one of the reasons I came back. Have a happy, memorable Centenary.

Shelley Ridler

1989
September 5th. Mrs Eileen Morrison, and Mrs Lisa Walker joined the staff. 384 children on the roll.

1990.

July 2nd. Mrs Feely appointed English coordinator. Mrs Slater appointed IT and science coordinator.

July 25th. Junior Sports.

This school year has seen many changes. We have made great efforts to meet the demands of the national curriculum, and I am greatly impressed by the commitment of the staff. Morale is high here, though it is fairly low in the profession at large. It is generally agreed that there is far too much change coming into quickly. This year we saw the beginnings of the local financial control of schools. It is more work at school and a few heads will once again become administrators.

Two senior staff leaving July -- Mr Pickford, who has been here 14 years and is to take up a post as senior lecturer at Chester College. Mr Hayward, my deputy, who is to become a senior lecturer at Manchester Polytechnic -- evidence of the high-quality training of staff and curriculum development, that they had been involved in.

September. Staff.
Mrs Morrison
Miss Lomas
Mrs Windebank
Mrs May
Mrs Clark
Mrs Slater
Mrs Wates
Mrs Feeley
Mr Blease
Mrs Naughton
Miss Rooke
Mrs Walker
Miss Hill
Mrs Owen
December 21st. End of term.

This is the last entry in the log book.

The school log book finishes in 1990.
There are lots of other memories posted on our website
www.manchesterroad.org.uk

One feature of the 1980's and 1990's was the annual pantomime often held on 3 evenings. These were ambitious productions and greatly enjoyed by all who took part. Mrs Evers must take a lot of credit for all her hard work in this department.

We have found some old videos of these productions and can transfer them to DVD. If anyone is interested in purchasing any of the following on DVD please send an order and money to the school office.

Price £6 (Please add £1 if you want us to post it to you) Cheques made payable to Manchester Road Primary School

School concert	1985
Aladdin	1994
Cinderella	1995
Sinbad	1996
Snow White	2001
Aladdin	2002
Cinderella	2003
Sinbad	2004

If anyone has videos from missing years they could lend us we will make a copy and give you one copy on DVD free.

Memories from Mrs Owen

I am very pleased to have been asked to contribute some of my memories of Manchester Road School for a book that will celebrate its Centenary.Manchester Road was, is ,and always will be a great school! I have met an ex-pupil ,now living in South Africa ,who always visits the school when he comes back to Droylsden to see friends and family...that's how special it is to him and I'm sure many others feel exactly the same.

I started teaching at the school in 1981 which was when the ' Infant ' and 'Junior ' departments were amalgamated. This was ,of course, a big change for everyone but, as usual, most people did their best to adapt to the change in spite of the many challenges involved.

It was great for me to be able to teach ' year six ' ,my favourite year group again because , due to a lack of job opportunities , I had had to teach in a variety of secondary school throughout Tameside for the previous three years and although all the schools made me very welcome , I missed the wider variety of subjects taught at Primary School.

My fondest memories of Manchester Road are being involved in the annual Christmas Concert .It was great to see all the talent on show and it was fun when we used to dance ' back stage ' behind the curtains trying to make as little noise as possible!! Mrs. Turner and Mrs. Shaw were formidable with the stage curtains...no -one got through by mistake !

Another memory is of the creativity and involvement shown by children and their families when we had competitions..Easter Egg displays , Poetry Writing , Art Competitions ,Fancy Dress ...to name but a few ...all produced amazing results and helped to make these activities so successful.

I would like to thank both ex- pupils ,their families and staff for some very happy memories and to wish present pupils , staff and associates every success in the future...you certainly deserve it !

Mrs. B. Owen Teacher at Manchester Road 1981-2005

Memories from Miss May
My Name is Sara Mannion, formally Miss May, and I taught at Manchester Road from 1988 to 1992 in Year One. I was taken on as an NQT at the same time as Tracy Hellewell, we were both young blonde Yorkshire girls, (don't know if that has any relevance!!) I have very fond memories of my time in Droylsden; the infant staffroom was run efficiently by June Saxon, always a hot drink waiting for you, and we were never late with the tea money! We had a good laugh together. At that time the staff consisted of Jill Lomas,& Joy (?) followed by Eileen Morrison in Rec, us two in year one and Pru Clark and Chris Reilly in Year two. Alison Cooke came in like a breath of fresh air from Wednesday to Friday.

My first impressions were mainly of the horrible off classroom toilets! I remember mopping spilt milk as a daily occurrance and the smell of the mop and toilets was not good, especially in the summer. We had to collect dinner money in a special tin on Mondays and it always came back smelling of smoke from the office. We were a bad example then with lots of the staff being smokers.

For the first year or so we had school dinners in the classroom so we had to pack up early while the tables were set, very noisy it was, and after lunch you had to cope with spilled peas and custard and the smell of cabbage in the class. It was great when the new dining tables and flight trays started to be used. Frank Blease used to come over and practice piano in the hall every lunch time too.

I had a class goldfish called Bubbles, which the children got to see very rarely because I hardly ever got to clean the tank.
The staff were very sociable and we used to go for pub lunches on a Friday, we used to get 1 and 1/2 hours in those days. Staff brought in cakes when it was their birthday, or fruit salad when we were dieting!
We had good trips out to Thurstaston on the Wirral where we went beach combing and Blackpool Zoo, and a memorable one to the transport museum where we got to eat our lunch on ancient buses.

I have photographs somewhere of the staff dressed as pirates for comic relief, and me dressed as a teddy bear for a teddy bears picnic on the yard.

One year I did a topic based on "The Enormous Crocodile", and the classroom was transformed into a jungle with dangling models every where. I'm not sure what the cleaners made of it all!

The Christmas parties were always good. We made table decorations and place mats for every child. The children got changed into party clothes at lunch and then we played games like Looby Loo and musical mats until tea time. Each parent brought in items of food on a special list and June made jelly and sandwiches with them. It was always the same and ran like clockwork.

Chapter 7 The New Millennium. 2000-2007 and beyond.

This short book shows some of the long and proud history of Manchester Road Primary School. We have seen glimpses of life in our school over the last 100 years. It is only right that we should finish by giving a voice to some of the present pupils of Manchester Road School

My School by Eleanor Sutcliffe

There's a big red building at the end of my road
My school.

It has lots of doors and windows
My school.

There's a sea of grey, with lots of giant coloured pencils in the playground
My school.

There are 14 classrooms and 2 big halls
My school.

There are lessons to listen to and games to play
My school.

There are books to read and books to write in
My school

I go to the big red building at the end of my road every day
My school.

Manchester Road Song

We are the children at Manchester Road
And our school is one hundred years old
Hop, skip and jump, now shout out hooray
Because today is Centenary Day.   Amy Quinn Year 4

Chorus
Manchester Road is a hundred years old
It stays standing through the hot and cold
We've got the eco flag on the pole
This is our song about Manchester Road.   Nicole Lunt Year 6

From the past until the present day
From the past until the present day

100 years this school has been here
We like it so we have no fear
We have got a football team
The joining hands are our theme.   Emma Thomas Year 6

Chorus

One hundred years ago they got the belt
Because of how they behaved or spelt
In school today the belt is gone
We guess today it is more fun.   Jessica Fisher Year 6

Chorus

Manchester Road is the best
We have to be quiet during a test
Mr Wynn runs the school
Don't dare dis him because he is cool.   Jake Mortimer Year 6

Chorus x2

Appendix 1 Alphabetical list of pupils 1907

Surname	first name	date of birth	parent/guardian
Adams	Olive	1895	Thomas
Adams	Ivy	1897	Thomas
Adams	Doris	1899	Thomas
Aldred	Hannah	1896	Hugh
Ashcroft	Fred	1894	John
Ashcroft	Minnie	1897	John
Atkinson	John	1895	Julias
Atkinson	Lilly	1894	John
Atkinson	Jason	1899	James
Bacchus	Herbert	1896	Herbert
Bacchus	Joseph	1899	Joseph
Bacon	Fred	1897	Thomas
Bacon	Ernest	1899	Thomas
Baguley	Annie	1896	Edmund
Baguley	Arthur	1897	Richard
Baguley	Harold	1899	John
Ball	William	1895	Edward
Bannister	Charles		
Barlow	John	1897	John
Barlow	Percy	1898	
Barlow	James	1899	Robert
Barrow	J.H	1896	John
Barton	Sydney	1895	Joseph
Beasley	Lilly	1896	Fred
Beasley	Gladys		
Beasley	Clara	1898	Edward
Bell	George	1898	William
Binns	Walter	1894	Matthew
Binns	Sydney	1897	Matthew
Binns	Peter	1899	Matthew
Birch	Arthur	1895	Emma
Blackburn	John	1897	John
Booth	Clara	1894	James
Booth	Hettie	1898	Novello
Bottomley	Annie	1896	Harry
Bradley	Edith	1899	Elizabeth
Brelsford	Edith	1895	Bertha
Brierley	John	1896	Thomas
Brierly	Sty	1894	John
Broadhurst	Alice	1898	Samuel
Brooksbank	Ernest	1896	John
Brooksbank	Fred	1897	William
Brooksbank	Harold	1899	William
Broom	Ada	1900	William
Broome	Mary	1894	William
Broomhead	Florence	1896	John
Brown	Frank	1896	Frank
Bruce	Evelyn	1900	Walter
Burgess	Thomas		Thomas
Burns	Harold	1900	John

Bussey	Harold	1897	Charles
Bussey	Dorothy	1899	Charles
Butcher	Charles	1894	charles
Butterfield	Minnie	1895	
Butterfield	Ernest	1898	Albert
Butterfield	Albert	1895	Albert
Buxton	Gladys	1898	Thomas
Caldwell	Arthur	1896	Daniel
Caldwell	Harold	1899	Daniel
Carpents	May	1897	John
Cartwright	Ethel	1896	Fred
Cecil	James	1898	James
Chadwick	Elsie	1898	Robert
Chapman	Harold	1900	Frank
Chappells	Annie	1898	George
Chappells	Florence	1897	George
Chappells	Maria	1896	George
Cheetham	F.W	1893	Chas
Cheetham	Vera	1899	James
Chipchase	George	1896	Fred
Coates	Arthur	1899	Arthur
Code	Harold	1896	John
Collier	Alfred	1898	Walter
Collinge	Elizabeth	1894	Thomas
Collinge	Robert	1898	Thomas
Collins	James	1895	John
Collins	Adelaide	1896	James
Collins	Sydney	1898	Jack
Cooke	Wilfred	1899	Joseph
Corbishley	Lizzy	1897	James
Davies	Ada	1896	Richard
Davies	Kate	1896	William
Davies	Sarah	1898	Edward
Dawson	George	1897	George
Dawson	George	1896	James
Dawson	Mary	1897	Joseph
Day	John	1896	Charles
Dellow	Sydney	1895	William
Dickens	Olive	1895	John
Dickens	Charles	1896	Walter
Dickens	Herbert	1898	Herbert
Dickens	William	1896	William
Dickens	Herbert	1897	John
Dickens	Jason	1899	Joseph
Dickens	Charles	1900	Harry
Dickin	Ivy	1897	Joseph
Dimelow	Robert	1895	William
Dimelow	Emily	1899	William
Docker	Ethel	1895	Elizabeth
Docker	Gladys	1898	Elizabeth
Donald	Lewis	1897	William
Douglas	James	1895	James
Dugdale	Alice	1895	Henry
Dunkerley	Wilf	1896	John

Eckersley	Madge	1898	Frank
Ecob	Ruby	1897	Thomas
Edgar	Doris	1896	Jas.
Edwards	Jason		Thomas
Ellis	Alice	1895	Albert
Ellis	Arthur	1898	Albert
Ellison	William	1898	Harry
Entwhistle	Lizzy	1896	Joseph
Etchells	William	1900	William
Evans	Winifred	1896	Lewis
Evans	John	1898	Lewis
Eyre	Elizabeth	1897	George
Featherstone	Harold	1894	Joseph
Featherstone	Albert	1898	John
Fielding	Mary	1895	
Fielding	Charles	1898	John
Finch	Lily	1895	Coruclius
Ford	James	1897	Thomas
Ford	Thomas	1898	Thomas
Forrest	Percy	1896	John
Foster	Emily	1894	Marg?
Foster	William	1896	Richard
Foster	Gladys	1898	Mary Ann
Foster	Elsie	1898	Richard
Frier	Richard	1895	Chas
Gansham	Alfred	1899	Charles
Gradwell	Elsie	1897	James
Green	Agnes	1895	Charles
Hackley	Leon	1894	James
Hadfield	Elizabeth	1896	James
Haigh	Ben	1898	Joseph
Hallsworth	Clarrie	1897	Samuel
Hargreaves	Harold	1896	Thomas
Hargreaves	Nelly	1899	Thomas
Harper	Fred	1895	Edward
Harper	Reginald	1899	Edward
Harrison	Lilly	1898	David
Hartley	Agnes	1896	William
Hatton	Una	1897	Jabez?
Haughton	Lizzy	1898	John
Hawley	Arthur	1894	Edward
Haywood	Lizzy	1896	Thomas
Headlam	Jessie	1896	jesse
Hibbert	Joseph	1895	Joseph
Hibbert	Harold	1897	Fred
Hickey	Alfred	1899	
Hickie	Anne	1894	William
Hickie	Stephen	1895	William
Higginbottom	Harold	1898	Joseph
Hilton	Arthur	1895	Jack
Holgate	Harold	1898	William
Holland	Aimee	1895	
Hollingworth	Annie	1897	Arthur
Hollingworth	Alex	1894	Alexander

Hollingworth	Edith	1895	Alexander
Hollingworth	Bertha	1898	Alexander
Hollingworth	Jason	1899	Robert
Holmes	Charles	1893	Geo Wm
Hopkins	David	1897	Richard
Hopwood	James	1899	James
Horrocks	Ethel	1900	George
Hughes	Thomas	1896	John
Hyatt	Winnifred	1896	Fred
Hyatt	Gert.	1898	Fred
Hyde	Charles	1894	Abraham
Hyde	Robert	1898	Abraham
James	Stanley	1897	John
James	John	1899	John
James	Harold	1899	James
Jones	Thomas	1895	Owen
Jones	Ernest	1894	John
Jones	John	1893	William
Jones	Bertha	1897	William
Jones	Lilly	1899	William
Kay	George	1899	John
Kendall	Ada	1895	Samuel
Kennedy	Dora	1895	David
Kennedy	cranmer	1899	Cranmer
Kerr	Edith	1895	John
Kerr	Arthur	1897	John
Kerr	Harold	1898	Charlotte
Kerr	James	1898	John
Kimber	Arthur	1899	Charles
Kimber	Edith	1896	Charles
King	Harold	1896	Phillip
Kitson	Henry	1897	Harry
Knowles	Norman	1898	Harrold
Lawson	Joe	1896	Herbert
Lawton	John	1896	Edgar
Lawton	Maggie	1898	Herbert
Lawton	William	1898	James
Leah	Ada	1899	John
Lee	Harold	1897	Thomas
Lee	Wilfred	1899	Thomas
Leigh	George	1895	Ellis
Lindley	Archibald	1896	William
Lloyd	Olive	1896	William
Lloyd	Annie	1897	William
Lloyd	Jane	1900	William
Lomas	William	1897	John
Longsden	Jason	1896	John
Longsden	William	1898	Walter
Longsden	Edith	1899	John
Lorrudes	Harv.		
Lowe	William	1899	Ralph
Lucas	Arthur	1896	George
Lucas	Jack	1898	George
Lunn	George	1898	George

Lyon	Harold	1895	Harry
MacGuire	Thomas	1898	John
Mafwell	William	1898	ellen
Makin	David	1899	James
Markham	Minnie	1895	Thomas
Marshall	Jason	1899	James
Marsland	Harold	1897	
Marsterson	John	1898	John
Mason	Albert	1896	Joseph
Mason	John		
Masterson	Ethel	1896	John
Mather	George	1900	
Mather	Thomas	1899	James
Matthews	Lucy	1900	Sarah
McDuggan?	Jem	1895	
McGuire	Harold	1898	John
McVeaty	Phillip	1895	John
McVeaty	Ernest	1898	John
Mellor	Elizabeth	1895	Thomas
Mellor	Charles	1899	Thomas
Mellor	Jack	1898	John
Mercer	Mary	1894	Thomas
Mercer	Elizabeth	1898	Thomas
Monks	Peter	1899	Peter
Morgan	Arthur	1895	William
Morgan	William	1894	William
Morris	George	1899	William
Nadin	Eunice	1899	James
Naylor	May	1899	John
Newton	Minnie	1895	James
Newton	Elsie	1897	Walter
Newton	Bertram	1897	Thomas
Newton	James	1898	James
Nield	Gert.	1897	James
Nuttal	Archibald	1896	Samuel
Oldham	Ethel	1895	James
Parrish	Harold	1898	James
Parrott	Elizabeth	1896	Henry
Parrott	hy	1898	Henry
Pearson	Harold	1895	Hannah
Pearson	Elsie	1897	David
Pearson	Ralph	1898	
Pearson	Ernest	1900	William
Percy	Florence	1895	John
Percy	John	1898	John
Percy	Samuel	1900	John
Perry	Herbert	1900	harry
Pilling	Priscilla	1895	Thomas
Potter	George	1896	Joseph
Potts	Mary	1899	Harry
Poyser	Mary	1894	Thomas
Poyser	Mary	1898	Thomas
Priestnall	William	1895	William
Profit	James	1894	Henry

Profit	Thomas	1895	Harry
Richmond	John	1898	John
Ridgeway	Edward	1897	Theodosia
Ridgeway	George	1896	Thomas
Ridgeway	Nelly	1898	Thomas
Roberts	John	1895	John
Robertson	hy	1900	Fred
Rooney	Marg.	1895	James
Rose	Clara	1895	Charles
Rose	Edward	1899	Charles
Royle	Thomas	1897	Thomas
Ryder	Rose	1895	Joseph
Ryder	Harold	1898	Joseph
Sanderson	Minnie	1897	William
Scotson	John	1895	John
Seel	Ada	1895	Hannah
Selby	James	1897	James
Shenton	Ernest	1898	Elisha
Shipley	Edward	1899	Walter
Silcock	Nelly	1896	Joseph
Silcock	Robert	1895	Joseph
Simon	Lizzy	1896	Hugh
Simon	Samuel	1895	Thomas
Simpson	Ethel	1894	James
Smith	Joshua	1896	William
Smith	Frank	1896	William
Smith	Thomas	1897	Robert
Smith	Norman	1897	John
Smith	Florence	1899	William
Smith	Fred	1898	John
Snelson	Fred	1899	Herbert
Stanfield	Harold	1895	Frank
Starr	Ernest	1896	James
Starr	Albert	1899	Thomas
Steadman	Florence	1895	Jarvis
Stewart	George	1898	William
Stopford	Lev	1894	John
Strange	Lilly	1897	Harriet
Sul	Harold	1896	Herbert
Sul	James	1899	Herbert
Sullivan	Frank	1896	John
Sullivan	John	1898	John
Summer	Selina	1896	Henry
Summer	Henry	1897	William
Summer	hy	1899	Henry
Swindells	James	1897	James
Swinfield	Alfred	1898	Alfred
Sykes	David	1897	William
Sykes	Norman	1897	William
Taylor	Gladys	1895	William
Taylor	William	1895	John
Taylor	Frank	1898	Joseph
Taylor	Wilfred	1898	Charles
Taylor	Emma	1894	John

Temple	Robert	1895	John
Tomlinson	William	1895	William
Tomlinson	Fanny	1898	William
Tonge	Orlando	1896	William
Toop	Annie	1899	
Torkington	Alice	1898	George
Torkington	Thomas	1899	Thomas
Towler	Florence	1894	William
Towler	Alwyn	1896	William
Travis	Wilf	1894	John
Turner	Harold	1895	Thomas
Turner	Emma		Thomas
Vagg	Elsie	1897	Edwin
Vagg	Hannah	1899	Edwin
Viney	Lillian	1895	Henry
Viney	Harold	1897	Henry
Wainwright	Susan	1895	Peter
Wainwright	William	1897	Peter
Wainwright	Lizzy	1897	Peter
Walker	John	1898	John
Walker	Bert.	1898	George
Walker	Ethel	1899	Frank
Walker	Barbara	1897	John
Walker	Frances	1895	John
Walker	Annie	1900	George
Walker	James	1896	Thomas
Warburton	Elizabeth	1896	George
Warburton	Jason	1899	George
Waring	Isabella	1899	Fred
Warrington	Elsie	1894	Alfred
Warrington	Doris	1896	Alfred
Wastall	John	1900	Thomas
Watson	John	1894	Arthur
Watson	Sydney	1898	charles
Webb	Dan	1896	James
Welden	John	1897	John
Wernyss	John	1896	James
Wharmley	James	1897	Samuel
White	Harold	1901	Thomas
White	Emily	1900	Robert
Whiteley	Saul	1894	George
Whiteley	George	1897	John
Whitmore	Norman	1897	Charles
Whittle	Ernest	1894	Frank
Widdowson	Edith	1897	William
Widdowson	Jessie	1899	George
Wilkinson	John	1894	John
Wilkinson	Gert.	1897	John
Wilkinson	Arthur	1896	Rebecca
Wilkinson	James	1896	John
Wilkinson	Thomas	1897	John
Wilkinson	Laura	1898	John
Williams	Sarah	1893	Samuel
Williams	Samuel	1897	Samuel

Williamson	Samuel	1896	Samuel
Winterbottom	Jane	1894	Edward
Winterbottom	Charles	1897	Edward
Withington	John	1895	Joseph
Withington	Laura	1895	Walter
Wood	Lizzy	1898	Walter
Wormald	Jack	1900	
Worsley	Jack	1900	William
Wrigley	Arthur	1895	John
Wrigley	Mary	1897	Walter
Wrigley	Emily	1899	John
Yarlett?	Joseph	1896	William
Yates	Herbert	1899	David
Yeomans	Joseph	1898	Harry

Many thanks to all those who contributed to this book.

Thanks to Susan Piper and Shelley Ridler for proof reading.

Thanks to all the ex-pupils who lent photographs or sent in their memories.

Thanks to the current children of Manchester Road for all their wonderful art work.

We look forward to the publication of the next instalment of the history of Manchester Road School in 2107!

If you have any further information you are welcome to send them to the school. Copies of all information will be deposited at Tameside Local Studies Library.

We have organised a Centenary Day for July 14th 2007. We hope you get the chance to attend. Look out for more details on our website.

www.manchesterroad.org.uk

Printed in Great Britain
by Amazon